Servant Leaders, Servant Structures

Elizabeth O'Connor

Potter's House Bookservice

1658 Columbia Road, NW
Washington, DC 20009

To the brave,
beautiful and diverse people
of Adams Morgan

The Potter's House Bookservice
is deeply grateful for those donors
who have made this edition possible.

Contents

Preface

In 1952, when I was one and thirty and new to Washington, D. C., two friends invited me to visit a class that Gordon Cosby was teaching at The Church of The Saviour. I was fond of these friends and in the debt of their love, so out of respect for what was important to them I went to visit the church that they were excited about and described as "different." I remember trying to take care of my resistance by telling myself, "What are you worrying about? It is only one evening to kill."

Gordon's class was my first introduction to the Sermon on the Mount. I listened spellbound. I had not been reared in a church and had not learned from Christian friends or my contacts with churches the revolutionary nature of the Gospel. I found it good news, foretelling a world of justice and caring, where the last were first, and everyone was needed and wanted and had a life to celebrate at the end of the day. Gordon suggested that members might want to help build the community toward which the sermon pointed. This was exactly what I wanted to do, though I was quite aware that a people committed to healing and beauty might have to make sacrifices and suffer. What I did not know then was the nature of that suffering, how wounded each one of us is, and how great is the task of loving ourselves and loving others. When the class was over someone asked me to sign the guest book. I hesitated, thinking I am no guest in this house. I signed, nonetheless, to record the date.

Almost forty years have gone by since that night. The Scriptures in my hands still seem new, and do their greening work. I also have the distinct impression that

The Church of The Saviour is all new—perhaps because it, too, seems to be setting out on yet another stage of its journey. Over the years I have tried to give readers a glimpse of a community as it struggled to take seriously the Sermon, and I have taken up that same work once again for this book. The first chapter was gleaned from my introduction to the first edition of Gordon's *Handbook for Mission Groups*, and the second from *The New Community*, a book I wrote in 1975. The third gives a hint of what has happened since then. The reader will be able to note through all three chapters a deepening and expanding of the concepts of servant leadership.

I want to thank my friends for all the assistance they gave. Marcy Porter researched the permissions and typed the first two chapters which Toni Wren entered into a computer. I wrote the third directly on a new Macintosh Classic given to me, together with a printer, by friends who wanted to make writing easier for me. John Tuohey was the overseer of this first publishing effort of the new Servant Leadership School described in the book.

Dorothy Devers, the author of *Faithful Friendship* and the editor of my books, was undoubtedly hoping that she might be replaced by the skills of the new technology I was mastering. That possibility, however, never existed. No computer will ever have her understanding of the well-designed sentence, not to mention the generosity of spirit required to perfect the work of another.

The cover and book design are the work of Laurie Swindull.

The publisher's logo on the back cover and title page is of Jimilu's bronze *Parable* which stands on the sidewalk in front of the School. The work is her companion piece to the figure of the *Servant Christ* across the street in front of our medical facility for homeless men. When Jimilu was placing this new figure of the teaching Christ on our ghetto street she was aware that passersby averted their eyes as though art was something not intended for them. Finally a woman stopped and asked, "How long is he going to be here?"

"Oh, he's going to live here," Jimilu replied. "He is here to stay."

"Well, then," said the woman, "I will take a look."

The photograph of the stained glass window on the cover was taken by David Welsh. The window is one of twelve, created by Gregory Cary and Bentley Roton of Woodstock, New York, to frame the entrance to the Servant Leadership School. The work is entitled *Celestial Journey*. The same artists created the stained glass windows in the chapel of the School. They have named their new work *Epiphanies: intuitive perceptions of the essential meaning*. In talking of these windows the artists expressed the hope that they would give to those in the room their own experiences of Epiphany—"moments of discovery, flashes of recognition." The words went to my own heart. Perhaps theirs is the wish of each of us— that the things that we do in life may in some way be the bearers of the eternal.

1

The Laying of Foundations

Roots of a Call

As a teenager Gordon Cosby stood on the street corners of Lynchburg, Virginia, passing out the Gospel of St. John and asking permission to speak with passersby about Jesus Christ, while all the time there grew in him doubts that this was the best way to share his excitement about the faith.

A childhood mentor, Graham Gilmer, filled his imagination with stories of the second coming. When Reverend Gilmer met him on the street he would point one finger upward, lean toward Gordon and say, "Maybe today..." He would conclude their conversations with "See you next week, Gordon...unless the Lord should come before we meet." This expectation was a part of the Southern church which nurtured its people in doctrine, Scripture, and hymnody. Six weeks of every summer Gordon went to an intensive Bible school where he was given reams of Scripture to memorize, and a gold star when he succeeded in memorizing more than anyone else in the group. Even today from time to time he takes up again this memory work, choosing a chapter from Ephesians, or a passage from the current study of the groups. More often he is memorizing a Psalm. He feels that this is a way to care for his own life and keep it steeped in the deepest mysteries of the faith.

All through his childhood he went on Sunday mornings to the Rivermont Avenue Baptist Church with his father, who was a confirmed Baptist and a deacon in the church. In the evening he went with his mother to the Presbyterian Church where Mr. Gilmer was the pastor.

He moved easily back and forth between these two congregations, absorbing with extraordinary equanimity the more fundamental, dispensational approach of his mother's church and the more liberal, patient and inclusive strain of his father's. When Ernest Campbell became the minister of the Baptist Church and moved into the manse with his wife and three children, Gordon found in the midst of this family a special home for his heart and mind. Dr. Campbell put the fifteen-year-old in charge of the young "Royal Ambassadors," while Mother Campbell favored his dramatic productions and other imaginative pursuits. His own home had always encouraged his adventuring and now, when the teenage years imposed on him the crucial task of establishing a new relationship with his parents and world, he found himself moving in the warmth and support of the family in the manse. Often a companion and always his admirer was ten-year-old Mary, the younger daughter in the Campbell family.

When Gordon was fifteen he and an older brother stumbled on a one-room church in the foothills of the Blue Ridge Mountains, about four miles from their home. When they discovered that it belonged to a black congregation that had no minister, they offered their services, and were later invited to preach. Gordon gave the trial sermon that first Sunday. When the service was over they were both asked to return. They preached in that church every Sunday for the next two years, during which time the membership swelled to forty. They were followed in their pastorate by two younger brothers. A first congregation must surely have a larger responsibility than is usually acknowledged for the response to, and care of a young minister. This little mountain church encouraged the gifts of their youthful pastors. They punctuated Gordon's sermons with their amens and in one way or another let him know that they were hearing what he said. One old man who sat at the end of the second row on the right interrupted each sermon at least once to shout, "Say it again, Brother. Say it again!" In the young preacher grew up a confidence that was never to leave him, a confidence in the power of the Word, and in himself as a proclaimer of that Word.

After high school he went to work in his father's savings and loan company to be groomed for a place in the business. All of his free time was spent in the activities of the church or at the manse. Around the Campbell's kitchen table or in the living room where young friends gathered, the talk more often than not turned to the church. These were the hours that excited Gordon and helped him to decide that his father's business was not for him—that he was to be a minister. Something broke within him, so that later he was to describe call as "a sense of being dealt with by that which is ultimate, of knowing that one was born to this, that one has found one's place in the scheme of things—in salvation history."

Then he simply announced to his family that he was going to the seminary. "I did not go the usual route," he says. "If I had written ahead I don't think that they would have accepted me. I didn't have any credentials." Two years after he began his seminary training at Southern Baptist Theological Seminary in Louisville, he began his college work at Hampden-Sydney College, not far from Lynchburg. He was never able to put his roots down very deeply in either the seminary or the academic community. During this period he had become the minister of a church in a nearby railroad town, and being the minister to these people was always more absorbing to him. These were also the years that he courted Mary Campbell who had grown up at last and was enrolled in Randolph-Macon College. Despite these diverse activities, in 1942, four and one-half years later, he was graduated magna cum laude from the college and in the same year completed his seminary training and was ordained to the ministry. This was also the year that he and Mary were married.

Mary, beautiful and gracious, had a passion for the church that was like his own. She complemented his shy seriousness, and added to every church occasion the festive note, which was in part her reaction to paper plate suppers in church basements. One man said of The Potter's House whose decor she had helped to select, "It's the only place I know where the atmosphere takes care of you." This is true of all the rooms where she has been. Flowers stand poised in a special way, candles are always lighted and the music playing. One feels received by the room itself.

War Distills Mission

Gordon was serving a congregation outside of Washington, D.C., when he enlisted in the army and was sent overseas as chaplin of the 327th Glider Infantry Regiment, 101st Airborne Division. In the winter of 1944 in England and later, on the broken terrain of Belgium, he began to work with concepts of ministry that were to be built upon, deepened, and refined over all the years to come. Like every other regimental chaplain, he found himself responsible for the spiritual life of more than three thousand men scattered over great distances and almost always under threat of immediate death. In many other settings he was to reform and restate the questions he began to ask then: How does one build the church in these circumstances? How can one be the church?

Reflecting on those war years Gordon now sees that his situation then was not very different from that of the minister of any congregation made up of men and women who throughout the week are spread out over large geographical areas in widely divergent places of work, many of which are oppressive structures that rob them of their lives without their knowing. How can one person, or even a team ministry, be pastor and prophet to the members of a congregation with whom there is very little possibility of developing any kind of depth relationship?

Perhaps, in a way that might otherwise not have happened, the battlefields of Holland and Belgium drew into sharp focus for Gordon the questions with which every minister in some way struggles if he takes with any seriousness the building of the church. Knowing as he did that he could not minister in depth to even two hundred men in a stationary situation, Gordon was painfully aware of how impossible it would be to meet the desperate needs of thirteen companies in combat. He moved quickly and decisively to bring into being a little church in each of the companies.

First he identified the man in each company who seemed most spiritually mature and, in effect, ordained him to the ministry as the "sky pilot" for his company. He then began a miniature seminary to train these men for the ministry and to help them identify and name an assistant. Around these pairs of men formed small bands who became responsible for the spiritual life of the others in their companies.

These little churches within the companies became known as the Airborne Christian Church, for their congregations were the men who were to be dropped by glider on the world's battlefields. They were also the forerunners of the early Church of The Saviour fellow-ship groups which later evolved into mission groups. As often as war allowed, Gordon met with the newly ordained clergy in a training program that included the sharing of their ministries. Here also was the beginning of the design for our own Schools of Christian Living which, in effect, are seminaries for the training of the laity. Before the Airborne Church left the English countryside, it had outgrown its borrowed chapel and moved into a school gymnasium.

Other war experiences began to shape Gordon's ministry. There was the night that seven men were selected from his regiment to infiltrate the enemy lines, make observations, and feel out enemy strength. They were to leave one hour before midnight, stay until almost daybreak, and return if possible. In all likelihood only three, or two, or one would make it back, but such a mission would provide valuable information for the activities of the whole regiment the following day. In the "terribly long and terribly short" hours before eleven, most of the men came to talk with the young chaplain. They brought pictures of the babies that they had never seen and of their wives and mothers. They left with him trinkets and valuables to send home "in case," and always they put into his hands the address of some-one. They left scribbled notes. One man came to make his commitment to Jesus. He had put it off long enough. When eleven o'clock came they slipped off into the darkness.

Through the night Gordon waited and prayed and thought about all that might be taking place. As he listened to the sporadic barking of machine gunfire in the distance, he pondered the pictures of the families at home and hoped that God would comfort them when they got the news. He wondered if one or two would get back, and which ones they would be. And what of those who would die? Would the words that he had said to them have any meaning? Would the men be hindered or helped by those words when they stood in the presence of God?

That night he saw in those seven men Everyman and Everywoman. To none of us is given to know the time or the day, but the fact is ... "Maybe today." What does it mean for the church to be God's waiting people? Can our waiting be meaningful to others if we are not obedient while we wait? What does it mean to be "radically obedient?"—"radically committed?" What must our life style be?

It was almost dawn when a lone figure came through the morning mist. Gordon thanked God. And then came another, and yet another—until all seven were back. Such a reunion he had never seen. Their words tumbled over each other, "This is what happened to me." "Remember the first heavy exchange ...?" "How did you get by that sentry?" "This is the way it was ..." Seven dead men were alive—together again. There were new possibilities—things could be and happen once more.

That night became for him a parable of the church when she authentically gathers—"A group of people who have known that they were bound over to the power of death stumble on a treasure and that treasure is Christ. Miracle of miracles, doors that were closed open, gates of bronze are broken down. The words spill out as they try to tell one another what happened and how it happened, and of a Presence that was there."

All through the war the storytelling went on—more often when the men broke open C-rations and sat around eating and talking. Under the circumstances the usual defenses were gone, and quickly their conversations moved to a deeper sharing of themselves. When men are involved intensively in a common danger and do not know whether they will be around the next night, let alone the next week, they move with directness to satisfy the basic human need to be heard and to be known. Even gruff and untutored men listened without judgement and treated with tenderness each other's stories. Deep bonds of friendship were forged.

"We were drawing easily," said Gordon, "on the tremendous capacity for intimacy that is in each of us. I think this is why men sometimes romanticize war. We had that sense of community that we all yearn for and which many of these men had never known before and would never know again." It is not strange that Gordon Cosby has become the minister of a church whose unwritten covenant is that we will be enablers of each other in the telling of our stories.

In retrospect one finds other wartime experiences shaping Gordon's ministry. As he shared his understanding of Scripture with men from different expressions of the church and they shared with him out of varied experiences, their excitement about faith grew, and they knew once more an unexpected communion with one another. In those incredible moments when bread was broken and Christ stood in their midst, Gordon committed himself to becoming the minister of an unknown church that would be ecumenical in its spirit, in dialogue with all the churches—indeed, with all persons. He began to write home to Mary about the church that would later write into its member's commitment the words, "I will seek to be loving in all relations with individuals, groups, classes, races, and nations."

There was another who shared his dream of the church. While his regiment was still in England, he had become friends with Carl Werner, a large, vital and exuberant man, who was excited about what a community might be that took Christianity seriously. In their youthful enthusiasm it seemed to both of them that such a church would surely be empowered by the Spirit and infuse the whole of life. War would end. Men and women would put aside their arms—not because it was good strategy or something laid on their consciences to do, but because there would no longer be any need for weapons.

Werner wrote home to the girl to whom he was engaged, describing the church and suggesting that when the war was over they go to Washington and help to get it started. She not only wrote back yes, but said that she had a friend who was a potential donor. "Please send a prospectus." Gordon and Carl began work on it immediately and had the last draft almost completed when the invasion of Normandy began. After the landings were made, the intense fighting gave them no time to meet and plan the church. On the 16th of June, 1944, after days of fighting so fierce that they did not even try to see each other, Gordon picked up the casualty list and Carl Werner's name leapt out from all the others.

He spent that long and anguished day picking up bodies and loading them onto trucks and then unloading them in a designated field. Literally hundreds were piled in that field when he left with the alcoholic jeep driver for a lonely plain several miles away where he was to bury the dearest friend he had—the man who had befriended

with him a vision only dimly seen. In the spiritual
biography that he wrote years later he told something of
that day:

> Powerfully disciplined German Panzer troops were a
> few miles away, covering the Normandy countryside.
> With a damp New Testament in my hand opened at
> 1 Corinthians 15, save for one wizened alcoholic at
> my side, I was alone with an impossible dream. I
> knew the power of envy, a strange envy—the envy of
> my friend who was experiencing that which was
> denied to me for a while. I knew the power of the
> resurrection in the midst of unbearable loneliness and
> death. From that moment I knew that I could go on
> alone, if necessary. Faithfulness to what I had seen
> did not depend upon human support. Those agoniz-
> ing years were to make me singularly unconcerned
> with "success." Also I felt delivered in large measure
> from the fear of death. I was to be close to it many
> times during the next months, but its sting had been
> removed. The impact of this quality of experiencing is
> difficult to describe. It is so vivid and real afterwards
> it is as hard to disbelieve as before it was hard to
> believe. There is another realm! To touch it is to live.
> To become immersed in it is the only worthwhile
> pursuit, to give it to others, the deepest joy.

As the war went on and the 101st Airborne Division
moved into Germany, Gordon's uneasiness about the
larger church grew. Always he had felt the discrepancy
between what the church proclaimed and what she
embodied in her structure and life style. Now he was
observing day by day men who had been raised in all the
structures of the church, and yet were no more men of

faith than those raised outside her life. Under the pressures of fatigue and suffering, removed from law, order, family—the externals that in normal times keep things together for us all—they were confused and unable to detach themselves from the mores of a culture that sanctioned a different morality for war than for peace. It was a lawless morality that was to prevail for months in occupied Germany as though the peace had not been made. Again he was pondering the question of integrity of membership in the Body of Christ. What were the structures of the church that would so nurture men and women in discipleship that Christ would always have first priority in their lives no matter what the circumstances?

For two and a half years he and Mary had written back and forth to each other their dreams for the unnamed church, continuing by mail the conversation begun so long before around a kitchen table. Somewhere in their writing they began to feel that it would be much easier to fulfill their dream outside the denominational framework. For one thing, their church would have to be interracial and, for another, it would have to be free to experiment with new structures. Few churches of the 1940's allowed for either.

Building a Community

Fired by the vision of speaking a wondrous gospel through all the land, Gordon came home to begin The Church of The Saviour. He and Mary, together with Elizabeth-Anne, Mary's sister, who was in training at Garfield Hospital in Washington, D.C., began holding an evening vesper service for the nurses—one of their first efforts to let others know that they were "a church."

The School of Christian Living opened with one
student, a slow, conservative and unlettered lad whom
they had known in Madison Heights, Virginia. Billy had
no idea of what he was getting into when he moved to
the Washington area and looked up his old friends.
Ernest Campbell, at that time the minister of a church in
Alexandria, made the living room of his house available
as a classroom. For six months Gordon met with Billy to
teach him doctrine, Christian growth, and Bible; meantime they struggled to determine what gift he might
exercise on behalf of the new church. At long last they
enthusiastically decided that it was running the mimeo-
graph machine. Thereafter Gordon taught him as they
worked together on mimeographing. When the year was
over Billy was transferred by his employer to Iowa,
leaving Gordon to wonder whether that first lone recruit
might not have effected his own transfer in order to be
free of involvement in an enterprise that was always
slightly bewildering. In any case, Billy's departure did
not lessen the ardor of his instructor, who remained
firmly convinced that the school, or "little seminary,"
was essential training ground if the church was to have
an inward life and move with any force in the world.

That year with Billy was in its way typical of Gordon
Cosby's ministry. He had issued a call to church and the
Lord had sent one person; so he treated that uncom-
plicated youth as though the whole future of the church
depended on him. In time he was to believe even more
deeply in ordinary persons who, in turn, were to believe
more deeply in themselves. This is probably why the
community that has come into being under his leadership gives so little attention to credentials—a fact which
is at first disappointing to those who come presenting
degrees and programs to help us out of the trouble we

are forever in. In all the years that I have been in this community no one has ever asked me which college I attended, although ministers from other places inquire about this as well as about my theological training. I have to tell them that I did not make it very often to grade school, but that I put in four hard years in high school. When they indicate that this is very fine, I am never sure whether they are trying to communicate acceptance of me, or whether their attitude implies a widespread conviction that our educational institutions are failing to provide the training needed to conduct our affairs and build community—always a work of art. If we are to build the church we must each day learn things we were never taught.

Paradoxically, this community which takes so little notice of degrees gives inordinate attention to education. Five classes are still required for membership in the church: Old Testament, New Testament, Doctrine, Christian Growth and Ethics. In addition, in every eleven-week semester a half-dozen other classes dealing with some aspect of the inward-outward journey are offered. They vary in content and focus, and range all the way from "discovery of self" to journaling and contemplation. Classes are taught by those whose call and gifts identify them as teachers. They are always persons well-informed in a subject they have pursued because of an absorbing interest. We have discovered that people usually communicate well the subjects that have stirred something deep within themselves. The usual student-teacher relationship seldom prevails. Most of the classes are conducted in the manner of a seminar with each student presenting findings from the application of the week's assignment in the living out of his or her life.

Completion of two eleven-week classes in the school is a requirement for internship in one of the small groups. The fact that the five classes required for full membership take approximately two years always gives rise to the question, "How do you manage to find people who will go to school for that long a time?" The answer is that we do not try. The students who move through the school each year do not stop to consider that the classes are required for membership. They are not there to meet standards, but because it is a stimulating place to be. Most of us who have been in the membership for any length of time return to the school now and then for a new course that is being offered, or to review in our more "informed state" an old class.

When a person has had the equivalent of the subject matter covered in any one of the required courses, and if his small group concurs, we will waive the requirement for that class. The request, however, is seldom made. In the beginning we rather automatically gave special dispensation to ministers who came to be with us. After all, we reasoned, a person who has been to seminary and preached in a church would not need classes in New and Old Testament. We changed our attitude, however, when these same people later complained that they felt robbed—as though they had missed out on something intangible but essential for their belonging to the whole.

In the early days theology was taught and learned while the work of introducing prospective members to the community went on. The school assumed a more formal structure only as the church grew. One of the most powerful supporters was Mother Anne Campbell who was teaching a Bible class at her husband's large, conventional Baptist church. She talked so enthusiastically about the church that was getting underway that, with her encouragement, several good Baptists ventured over into the new fold, and then they, in turn, lured a few more. Elizabeth-Anne was also issuing frequent calls at Garfield Hospital, while Gordon shared his life and dream with every likely and unlikely soul that crossed his path. The street evangelist of Lynchburg now had as his mission field the unchurched of the nation's capital. Even so, at the end of the year the whole congregation numbered only nine.

Struggle for Integrity

These nine were bound together by a covenant written by Gordon's brother, Peter Cosby, and printed on a small blue card that each member was to sign and carry. Included were such high and lofty statements as, "I unreservedly and with abandon commit my life and destiny to Christ, promising to give him a practical priority in all the affairs of life." Through the years only a rare person ever questioned his or her capacity to fulfill the covenant. On the back of the card, however, were printed the disciplines that translated into specific and concrete terms the community's understanding of what that covenant meant. Over these more prosaic, more explicit statements there was to be a falling away of would-be members who felt some of the sayings to be too hard. The founding members, often petitioned to change them, could never bring themselves to do it. They had hammered out those disciplines in order to become the kind of community they envisioned. The disciplines also embodied their understanding of the nature of the church. They had included a discipline of praying because they understood the church of Jesus Christ to be a praying people. They had covenanted to meditate on Scripture every day because the church is a people informed and instructed by the word of God. They had agreed to give proportionately beginning at ten percent of their gross income because this was essential if they were to have a thrust into the world that would be exciting to them as well as to others. It early became evident that to reduce any one discipline was to reduce them all, for each individual struggled at a different point. One person who had difficulty with a set time of prayer would find the tithing concept quite acceptable, while another found the prayer discipline easy but the parting with money an unspeakable hardship.

The small fellowship was very early confronted with temptation from within their company. Their incomes were all meager. Elizabeth-Anne made $20 a month. Frank Cresswell was an intern doctor holding his young family together on $120 a month. Gordon was working part-time for a small Baptist church so that he would be free to spend the rest of his time with the new church. All were hampered financially—except for one member who, substantially employed, lent an air of financial respectability. He was the one who questioned the concept of "corporate disciplines" and "corporate re-sponsibility." It was then that the little group began to be aware of the costliness of its call. They had to examine at a new level their definition of church as a voluntary community with a clearly defined life style. They talked for hours and hours, confronted and questioned their own motivations and convictions, and named aloud their fears of destroying the delicate fabric of the fellowship in the name of building it. There was no short cut through the painful work of coming face to face with the knowledge that treasured friends whose call and commit-ment led them by a different path would have to be allowed to leave.

Perhaps the experience of those weeks instructed the little community to write into its constitution the principle of annual recommitment. They agreed that during the third week of each October, having reflected on the commitment they had previously made, they would, if they could, again sign the membership book. Then, on Sunday they would stand and say together the covenant beginning, "I come today to renew my commitment to this local expression of the church ..."

October came to be known as the month of "recommitment blues," a term that gives some hint of the work going on in our lives. Gordon Cosby was to say that this concept, perhaps more than any other, was the one destined to be the most helpful in retaining integrity of membership. It was, and still is, a time for raising into fuller consciousness the high call of God in Christ, and our commitment to live out that call in one particular segment of his church. We had structured into our lives a period of self-examination against the backdrop of the covenant we had made and the disciplines we had pledged ourselves to keep. Sometimes, when October came we were made aware that we had become lukewarm, were in the process of drifting away, and were in need of help.

Occasionally a person discovered that she or he really "wanted out" but was fearful of abandoning the community or of being abandoned by the community. However, moving out of membership at recommitment time rarely meant moving out of the church. Often a person has taken this step and then rejoined after an interval that can be very long or very short. Rather than a sign of defection, withdrawal from the membership is often a sign of health—a time when a person takes the distance needed for seeing again the choices that exist for renewing old covenants or making new ones. At the same time, the principle of annual recommitment offers recurring assurance that the members, in freedom, have bound themselves together under a covenant that not only describes who they are but also will help them in their journeying to where they want to be.

The community's first purchase was an old rooming house complete with housekeeper and several roomers who stayed on and were caught up in the contagious exuberance of the new occupants. The previous residents helped with the painting—and cast their lot with the odd but captivating band of newcomers. The question then was: Would there be money enough to buy the paint to carry on the next day's work? That question still comes up as paint is needed for the restoration of apartments in the inner city. We know now that the community being born then was always to smell slightly of turpentine and have paint on its shoes. For more reasons than one, one of its missions bears the appropriate name of Jubilee Housing.

In those days we were blissfully ignorant of the houses for which we were to be the agents of transformation. Only a few years went by before the first quarters were obviously inadequate, and we acquired a twenty-three-room house and began again to scrub, scrape and paint. This old Victorian mansion still remains the headquarters and place of worship for the whole community. The corporate indebtedness was huge. We were then about thirty-two persons, probably twenty of whom were employed, and we owed about one hundred thousand dollars. Our distinction at that time was that we probably had the highest per capita indebtedness of any church in the country.

Hart Cowperthwait

Headquarters for The Church of The Saviour is a twenty-three room mansion purchased in 1950 and converted to church use by the members.

The work of renovation on the new building was
scarcely completed when the group further increased its
indebtedness by the purchase of 176 acres of land in the
country. The membership had grown to thirty-six, and
there were another fifty or sixty persons taking classes.
Again there was a farmhouse to restore and the Lodge of
the Carpenter to build. The large living room, kitchen,
and dining room made it possible for eighteen persons to
make day-long retreat. As we became more involved in
the outward journey, it became more essential to give
equal attention to the inward journey, and we began to
think about weekend retreats that would give us more
time in the silence. Finally, we built behind the Lodge
overnight facilities for eighteen retreatants. Each room
has a single bed, a washbasin, a desk, two chairs, and a
lamp. All the windows look out on woodland.

As we grew in our understanding of silence, we gave
more emphasis to the contemplative life. When we
become too busy, Dayspring is always there as a reminder
that there is no true creativity apart from contemplation.

Struggle for Mission

The mission of the community now became the primary
issue. The gifts of teaching had been identified, and basic
classes were offered every semester. Church members
met in small fellowship groups committed to worship,
tithing, prayer, study, and corporate outreach. Not one
of them, however, was able to agree on what its outreach
would be. We sat in our little groups and discussed it
week after week, but all our prayer, imagining, and
investigation produced nothing which caught the common soul. We were slow to recognize that the very
diversity of gifts made it impossible to find a corporate

mission. One person would say, "Let's have a street music group." The next person would reply, "I'm tone deaf." Someone would suggest working with alcoholics, and another person would answer, "Not for me." The exploration went on and on, and it seemed there was always someone to put out the fire in another.

Somewhere in the midst of it all it became clear that there was only one way to solve our dilemma. If the church was to find servant structures, the small groups had to be formed around focused and defined missions with each mission also committed to an inward journey of prayer, worship and study. This concept seems very simple to us now, but in those early days there were no models and no guidelines, nor was there any confirmation of that toward which we struggled. Just about that time we came across what seemed like a very promising book. The writer was describing the very things we were committed to; more than that, he promised to offer help before he was done. Chapter followed chapter with no yielding of secrets. The pages were running out when the writer suggested that those wanting to pursue the matter further turn to the appendix. There one was advised to write to The Church of The Saviour in Washington, D.C.!

Gordon Cosby still feels that the churches, in their quest for structures that nurture life in people, must know that they are venturing into new territory, and that the resources for their exploration rest in the tremendous untapped potential of their own people. The difficulty is that we so often lack confidence in ourselves and in our companions and search for the answers in some other place.

The decision to abandon the small fellowship groups in order to form mission groups was again a tearing one.

For one thing it meant parting with those with whom we had shared the very depths of ourselves, and with whom we had deep bonds. Secondly, some of us were not at all convinced it was essential; and thirdly, there was really no place to go. When it came right down to it, we had never taken seriously our own responsibility to hear call and to issue it. At one point it seemed that we were all milling around in a kind of anguished confusion, as though we, too, had been brought out of Egypt to die in the wilderness.

In the midst of the confusion Gordon walked with the sureness of one headed for a far better place. He stopped to reason, comfort and confront, but there was no question as to the direction in which he was set. Furthermore, it seemed not to disturb him that some felt torn up and anxious. To him it was a highly creative time—all a part of breaking up camp and moving toward the Lord who waited outside the camp. "To be a disciple," he explained, "is to share in the life of which the Cross is the culmination. In the evolution of an individual, there is an inner work to be done, and that is always costly." In his preaching and in his conversation he was reminding his own little band that the call of God was a call to create a new kind of community that would be distinguished by its humanness. It would be so human that those in it would do whatever was needed so that everyone in the world might be free. He was reissuing the call to which we had first made response. Later he was to tell the moderators of newly formed mission groups, "A time comes in the life of every group when it loses sight of its goals and must choose them again. Your job will be to sound again the call, to be the bearer of the vision—articulating it in your own life and helping others to see it."

Elizabeth O'Connor

Gordon Cosby on the headquarter steps, 1975.

Waiting for Call

To help us through our impasse we formed classes in
Christian Vocation. In these classes we were taking a
deeper and longer look at the whole matter of call as
having to do with the transcendent—the being grasped
by that which is greater than we. We began with the
basic assumption of the New Testament that there was
no way to be the church except by the call of Christ, and
that there were a number of dimensions to this call:

First, to a relationship with the Father as intimate as
the one which Christ knew.

Second, to be persons in community with others
responding to the same call, surrendering something of
our authority that we might have a shared life and bring
into existence a new community where the nature of the
relationships would be such that each person would be
called fully into being.

Third, to an inward development—a call to change.
We were to overcome those obstacles in ourselves which
held us back and kept us from growing into the full
stature of Christ. The call of Christ was a call to die to
the old self in order to become the new creation.

Fourth, and not last, the call was to move out—to
discover where we were to lay down our lives—to take
up the stance of the suffering servant, and make witness
to the power of Jesus Christ's work in us.

The class dealt primarily with the fourth dimension.
If the church is a *sent* people, where was Christ sending
each of us? To what segment of the world's need were
we to make response? We began each session by sitting
for an hour in silence, feeling that if any word was being
addressed to us we had more opportunity of hearing it
in the stillness of our own souls. Part of the work of the

hour was to center deeply enough in ourselves to be in touch with our most central wish. Somehow we had then, and have now, the conviction that our wishes lie very close to "who we are" and what we are to be doing, and that to be in communion with them is to have a sense of being dealt with by the One who is Other.

We discovered in this class that too many of us had taken up our work without any sense of being called to it. "Vocation," Gordon said, "has the element of faithfulness to your own inner being. You are enhanced by what you do. Your own awareness converges with some need out yonder and intersects with it in such a way that you have the sense that you were born to this." Jesus said, "I must be about my Father's business."* He knew. His knowing was an inner one.

When the time of silence was over we timidly put forward any intimations of direction that had come to us. We were so uncertain and so consumed by misgiving that the question was inevitable: "Is not one's call often shot through with self-doubt?"

We decided that doubt is a dimension that oftentimes is there, and that there is a time to move on in spite of it. In fact, we agreed that if anyone were too dogmatic about call, he or she needed to question it because there is always the possibility of acting out of some compulsive need rather than genuine call. Frequently along with the call comes the feeling that one is not up to it. There is a sense of unworthiness in relationship to what one sees. "Who am I to be called to bring into existence anything so significant? Surely there are other people more qualified to do it." This is what Moses felt. He was forever protesting that Yahweh could choose someone better equipped for the job, someone who talked more convincingly than he did. Jeremiah said flatly that he

*Lk. 2:49, KJV.

was too young, even going to the extreme in that declaration, "'I am only a child.' But the Lord said, 'Do not call yourself a child; for you shall go to whatever people I send you and say whatever I tell you to say.'"*

All of us resist in some way the new thing into which we are drawn that demands a whole new dimension of creativity on our part. We do not want to be responsible in this way. "It may be," says Gordon, "that if a person responds too eagerly, he is not seeing the whole picture and is not aware of the problems of implementation, so that he goes into it with large areas of unconsciousness."

Despite our expectancy and all the assurance and encouragement we gave to each other, no one was addressed by a Voice, which is the real meaning of having a vocation. Perhaps it was because we were too disbelieving, or too unpracticed in the process in which we were engaged, or perhaps we were too literal in our understanding of call—expecting somehow that God was going to descend out of heaven and summon us as we sat with heads bowed. Actually call was to come to most of us through the ordinary events of life, which were to be extraordinary events because we brought to them a new quality of asking and listening.

In the spring of that long year Gordon and Mary made what might have been a routine trip to a church in New England where Gordon gave the Lenten address. They found the atmosphere in the church cold and the congregation unbending, and they left with a feeling of wanting to put that whole, dark church far behind them. They drove for a long distance, before they stopped at a country inn and were given the last available room, which happened to be above the tavern. The noises from that tavern drifted up to them and disturbed their sleeping, but somewhere in the night Gordon thought,

*Jer. 1:6-7, NEB.

"Christ would be more at home in that tavern than back in the church we just left."

The next morning he and Mary had breakfast in a small restaurant across the street from the inn, and there again the friendliness and warmth made him think, "Christ would be more at home in this restaurant than in the church." They went home to tell the class in Christian Vocation that a way should be found to take the church to the restaurants of the city. Out of the discussion that followed emerged the idea of a coffee house and, in the naming of it, call was heard. Gordon and Mary and several others knew that they were called. Some felt that it was not for them, but encouraged the sounding of the call in the larger congregation. Twelve people responded, and the mission was under way.

When The Potter's House finally opened a year later we had been joined by others, and with everyone working two and sometimes three times a week we were able to keep open on six nights. The disciplines for members and intern members were decided upon and within a few months there were eight or ten people to staff each of the nights and thus each night had its own mission group. Here we were to develop and expand the concept of gift-evoking that has become so central to our life. People who had not been able to understand what a coffee house had to do with the church caught the idea the moment they went through the doors. The Potter's House, on that ghetto street, remains a sign of hope— "its own excuse for being."

In the meantime others began to hear call and to issue call, and new missions were born. Three were committed to keeping strong the home base and equipping us for ministry. The first of these was the Retreat Mission Group, which had among its responsibilities deepening the community's life of prayer and the nurturing of the mission groups in the whole concept of retreat. Then there was the group that had as its concern the children of the church. Another group took on the responsibility of the School of Christian Living, incorporating into that structure the whole concept of mission as it was being developed. Our sermons, classes, and conferences were all concerned with helping others to hear call and discern gifts. We found ourselves so often asking, "What is it that you want to do now that you are six?" "What would you like to do now that you are fifty and the children are away and you have the new gift of time?" "What do you want to do now that you are eighty, and have the resources of a whole lifetime to bring to every work?"

"What would you like to do?" is a question we still ask indiscriminately—of the very young and the very old, of poor and rich, oppressed and oppressors, and then we listen very carefully and take with utmost seriousness what a person says.

As more people began to hear call, more missions came into being. These calls were first explored in the small community of one's close friends, and later in the larger community. We began to know that it can be painful to have one's vision tested by people who are not friendly to it, or who ask what seem to be unimportant questions. We soon discovered, however, that the corporate input forced us to refine and sharpen our thinking and enlarge the dream. In the end we worked out a procedure requiring every mission to be confirmed by the Church Council. This never meant to us that everyone had to be enthusiastic about every call.

Oftentimes we have had to be willing to let another move even when we have large reservations. Our learning to do this with a certain degree of ease, probably more than any other factor, accounts for the proliferation of mission groups in the community of The Church of The Saviour. This does not mean that we easily deal with anxiety, angry feelings and ego needs. Some have learned slowly to reason with unreasonable fears, and for them the pain has been very great. Others have discovered that there is nothing lonelier in all the world than to live in the midst of those who know community and to feel in one's own heart estranged, or to be at the center of a gift-evoking group where there is no one to receive what one has to give, and from time to time some of us find ourselves in those desolate stretches of land. Always, too, we have found it incredibly hard to hold to the concept of the inward and outward journeys. We early discovered that not many persons want them both. Weighted heavily on one side or the other, most of us struggle intensely to keep these two dimensions in any kind of creative tension in our individual and our corporate lives.

A Mission is Defined

Every mission group has known not only its beginning excitement and small triumphs but its extremely difficult times. For The Potter's House one such time came in the spring of 1965. Having freely released a number of its people to follow other calls and to join new missions, it found itself understaffed. This made The Potter's House groups especially vulnerable to the arguments of those who wanted to help staff it without subscribing to all the disciplines or participating in the School of Christian Living. We were too often won to thinking that not everyone can travel the same path, and that some people were just too individualistic to subscribe to our recommendations. So we began to make exceptions, which we still do, but the exceptions became the norm, and the whole character of the evenings began to change. Fortunately, it didn't work very well. Group members were inconsistent in their attendance, and when they did come they ceased to find what had attracted them in the first place. Even the customers dropped away, and the receipts went down and put the whole enterprise in the red.

One weekday afternoon The Potter's House Council, made up of one member from each of the groups, met and accepted what was an astounding and risky recommendation. What Gordon in essence proposed was that we agree to close The Potter's House, that all persons then staffing it be released from their commitment, and that on the following Sunday a new call be issued, re-forming The Potter's House around highly disciplined groups.

"What if enough people do not respond?" we asked. "At least now we can keep it open, and try to work out something."

"I think that would be a mistake," Gordon replied. "If we do not make the issue sharp enough, it will have no teeth in it."

"But," someone said, "it is going to stir up a lot of feeling and anxiety."

Gordon thought that just might be a good thing. He felt that we had let the whole matter drift into the present state and that, although we had voiced concerns before, we had not dealt with them.

I can remember that afternoon: his lounging in the chair in a characteristic way, enjoying our surprise, and by his very attitude injecting expectancy and challenge into a meeting that was shrouded in gloom when it started. Before long we were caught up in what he was proposing, though I vividly recall thinking at the time, "We would never have come to this on our own," and wondering what made him so much freer and more trusting than most people seemed to be.

The answer may lie in what he said to a friend who asked him a question he is often asked, "What do you think the future of the church is?" He replied, "I have never had a helpful answer to that question. Have no idea. I do not know what the judgements of God are or what will be the breakthroughs of God's power." Then he stopped for a long pause and added, "I do not need the church to have a visible or successful future in order for me to feel safe as a person. I'm glad to leave it to God's sovereignty. It is his church—not mine."

The call that Gordon issued that Sunday morning was to a more rigorous and disciplined inward journey than any of the small groups had corporately adopted. The time that we set aside each day to work on the disciplines was increased from a minimum of thirty minutes to fifty minutes. Three new disciplines were added to those that the membership kept: daily writing in a journal, a report of accountability to be made each week to the group's spiritual director, and a weekly day of fast. The day of fast has become an optional discipline, but most of the members now keep a journal on some consistent basis and write a weekly report for the group's spiritual director.

The call sounded by Gordon that Sunday came as good news to many, and The Potter's House entered into a whole new era of creativity. This was the year that the riots had been contained in the surrounding streets only by the threatening presence of a large police force. The groans of the oppressed were heard everywhere, and The Potter's House became the seedbed of new missions.

It was now open during the day, and it was also opening
every morning to give a hot breakfast to forty neighborhood schoolchildren, pending the time the local school
could expand its program. We bought a small house in
the neighborhood and initiated a program for senior
citizens that included a hot midday meal. Bit by bit we
were being freed from old ways and customs. We had
once claimed Thanksgiving and Christmas days for
ourselves and closed the doors to a lonely city. Somewhere along the way we began serving Thanksgiving and
Christmas dinners for all who would come. Many of our
families gathered up their own children and arrived
bearing armloads of food as well. Poor and rich, black
and white, well and sick, young and old were there, and
there was always enough for all who came.

The Covenant is Questioned

Our grappling with the disciplines was not over. So
many ministers look at the structures we have arrived at
and, with no idea of the pain involved, feel that it would
be so much easier to start out fresh and call a new
congregation into existence around a different understanding of church. They feel that in their own denomi-
nations a tremendous pressure is exerted to increase the
number of members. "Being the church," said one
young minister, "means doing something to bring more
people in. Success is not measured in faithfulness but in
how many names are on the rolls."

To fight for integrity of membership within existing
structures is certainly extraordinarily difficult, but there is
hardly any path that frees one from that struggle. In all
of us something powerful is at work which seeks to
remake the new concepts into the old. "Community"

can quickly be changed into "conformity," and "call" into "duty." I like in Exodus the statement that says, "God did not guide them by the road...that was the shortest; for he said, 'The people may change their minds when they see war between them, and turn back to Egypt.'"* It is so easy to turn back when conflict without or warring factions within threaten our peace.

And then there is the old monastic cycle: devotion produces discipline, discipline produces abundance, and abundance destroys discipline. The cycle moves inexorably on and tremendous effort is required to break its pattern when we come to the place where discipline is sliding.

Our own time of terrible crisis came in October of 1969. On the third Sunday of that month, for the first time in the twenty-two years of the church's history no one stood up to make his or her commitment. We did not follow the tradition of annually renewing our covenant because the fourth discipline, "Be a vital contributing member of one of the confirmed groups, normally on corporate mission," was in question.

We had had difficulty with this discipline before. In the spring of 1965 we had held a meeting of the members in which three persons presented the differing viewpoints. After several weeks of discussion, the fourth discipline was confirmed; exceptions, however, would be made for illness and for those who wanted to meet together to deal concretely and creatively with their everyday vocations as mission in the world. No effort was made to cover every possible exception since it was emphasized that flexibility and openness to the guidance of the Holy Spirit would always be the primary emphases in any decision, and that we could never insist on simple adherence to the law.

*Exod. 13:17, NEB.

We thought then that the matter had been settled, but four years later when we looked one day at our mission group rolls we had to face the fact that one-fourth of our members were in no group at all. Again, we came together to look at the painful matter of our division. Once more we gave over our congregational meetings to careful consideration of the fourth discipline. Recommitment Sunday was postponed until we arrived at a decision as to exactly what our commitment was to be.

The question was whether a part or all of the congregation would normally be on mission in membership structures which include the inward and outward dimension. It was obvious that there was a real difference in judgement at this point. Some felt that the inward-outward structure of the mission groups defined the church as a servant people called into existence to be the community for others. Many contended that this was too narrow a definition and that one was often better able to live out one's servanthood in individual mission. To this the cry came back, "Where then is the place of accountability? Where does one grapple with one's own darkness and gifts, struggle with being a person in depth relationship with others? Where does the church embody in her structures what she proclaims from her pulpit?" The reply came: "We could contain both emphases and let those who wanted the corporate dimension be in mission groups, and let the others live on a more individualistic basis."

Gordon said decisively that he did not believe that we could contain both viewpoints under the same organizational and institutional roof without seriously blunting and ultimately losing that which has been our peculiar vision. He further said that he did not believe additional dialogue would serve any constructive purpose. He reminded us that we were not at the beginning of the process, but at the end of one which had been going on for four years. He said that he felt that the question was not one of further defining our differences, but the more painful one of deciding what we were to do about our differences. "How do we free those with different calls to be faithful to those calls?"

When the long weeks of anguish were over, the fourth discipline was again reaffirmed. At least a half-dozen persons did not make their recommitment that day in late March. Some remain close and dear friends who continue to follow a costly and radical obedience to the Word, as they hear it, and one can only affirm that the task for any of us is to do the will of God and humbly to pray the prayer of Thomas Merton, "I do not see the road ahead of me. I cannot know for certain where it will end. Nor do I really know myself, and the fact that I think that I am following your will does not mean that I am actually doing so. But I believe that the desire to please you does in fact please you."

Every religion and every denomination is founded on a vision defined in disciplines that enable a people to move toward that which they see. Most of these disciplines make our own look shabby, but somewhere along the way they have been abandoned. They remain in the books, but are not taken with any seriousness. My guess is that our own experience gives glimpses of what may have happened. Because we do not want to exclude anyone, we bend to everyone's wish and in the end have no style of life which is noticeably different from that of any other grouping of people. We give no one anything to be up against. We have been transformed by the world—not by the secular outside us but by the secular within us, that part that believes so fervently that something can be had for nothing and that we should not have to choose.

What we did at that important juncture in our life was to face the importance of structurally implementing a description of "Who we are." "Verbal assent," said Gordon, "can mean little. The implementing structures are crucial." We ended up by saying that the members of the church would live out their lives in small groups on corporate mission. To drop out of a mission group would literally be to drop out of membership in the church.

The Council as the governing body of the church was reorganized as a "Mission Council," comprised of two representatives from each confirmed mission group, who served in rotating order for a period of a year. Representatives reported to their groups what transpired in Council meetings. Any decisions made were binding on the whole membership. When the Council determined that an issue was of such nature as to require confirmation by the total membership, a general congregational meeting was called.

Economics and Mission

After those days call was more often heard. Each year one or two new missions were launched. A common practice was to give our Christmas and Easter offerings to the newest of them, so that it would have seed money. Most of the missions were eventually able to support their own work. However, when the annual budget was planned, the individual groups, having carefully considered their needs, presented them to the budget committee.

Our mission group structures are tougher and more durable because they have had to cope with the financial dimension. A group responsible for its own finance is not likely to close shop for the summer or to show laxity in ways that it might if someone else were footing the bills. Furthermore, when the money is ours we relate to the whole sphere of economics in a way that would not otherwise happen. This became increasingly evident as our missions in the inner city placed us in the midst of the poor. We returned to our homes at night feeling less easy with our own life styles.

Our dis-ease was intensified in the fateful year of 1968 when rioting in our streets tore veils from our eyes, and let us see in searing ways some of the misery of the oppressed. We looked differently at the boarded-up apartment building a few doors from The Potter's House and all of the decaying firetrap apartments and row houses in neighboring streets where the poor lived in crowded, miserable rooms, existing in what one reporter called "Dickensian squalor."

As we came to see more clearly the faces of those submerged in the crushing poverty of our own city, it became obvious that only those engaged in the struggles of the poor were going to be able to speak to them any message of God's reign. Around the tables of The Potter's House the conversation often turned to what we might do. The group which staffed The Potter's House on Thursday night began to give their attention to the massive problem of inadequate housing. They began to talk about purchasing an apartment house in the street behind The Potter's House and working with the tenants to upgrade it without raising the rents. In those days the foundations were laid for Jubilee Housing and for missions in education, health care and job placement

that would come into being in the neighboring streets.
When spring came the members of the new Jubilee
mission group made the down payment on what would
be the first of nine slum buildings that it would purchase
and renovate in the years to come. Workshops in paper-
hanging, glass cutting, and plastering were scheduled, and
people who never in a million years would have seen the
inside of a slum apartment were engaged in the renovation of one.

Everyone's Gift Counts

Once a group came into existence, we struggled with
naming the gifts of the members. The naming of call and
the identification of gifts were soon extended to those
touched by the mission. We asked Mrs. Henry, who was
in our dinner program for the aged, "What would you
like to do?"

"Nothing," she replied. "Nothing is what I want to
do. For forty years I left home at 6:00 in the morning
and traveled by streetcar and bus so that I could get to
my place of work and have breakfast on the table by 7:30.
I cooked three meals a day for that family, did their
washing and cleaning, and reared their children. When I
finished their dishes at night I went home and had to do
for my own family. No, I don't plan to do nothing but
sit, and sit, and sit. I never want to work again."

We learned then that evoking the gifts of those who
live in the inner city asked something different of us.
Mrs. Henry would not easily believe that her gifts of mind
and spirit were needed in the liberation movement. Like
so many thousands of the urban poor, she had left her
rural home as a young person to pursue the promise of
work and a better life in the city. She no longer believed

Elizabeth O'Connor

Gordon Cosby and a young companion stop to confer as they work in the yard of a building they are helping to restore.

in much of anything. She did not think about salvation for herself or for anyone else. Vast numbers of the poor, however, had another attitude. They had a growing consciousness of their right to participate in the working out of their own destiny, and were forcefully, sometimes angrily, presenting their claims. Others, deprived of opportunity for creativity, initiative, and space in which to move and rest, experienced rage, apathy, or despair.

If the listening to call and the exercising of gifts were unfamiliar concepts in our middle-class congregations, they were stranger still to those in the inner city where choice so seldom exists. And yet, the calls to which we then responded were not issued from the pulpit. They were sounded by the oppressed on the streets of the city, in tenement buildings and rat-infested alleys. By their very presence the poor were asking that we do more than "sit, and sit, and sit." "Hear, you who have ears to hear, what the Spirit says to the churches!"*

In our small church community the mission groups began to multiply. They were structures that Gordon Cosby had helped to form and that were, in turn, forming him. Although his life was given to working with all the small groups, he was a member of only one, subject to its covenant, under the authority of those whose gifts had been confirmed, his heart and mind enlarged and stretched by commitment to the few. He was sometimes advised that his ministry would be increased if he divided his time equally among all the groups, but he remained unconvinced. He believed too passionately that strong leadership existed within all the groups. He was, however, and still is available to any group as guide and counselor. Sometimes he is called in at points of crisis to be a reconciler. More often he counsels a group in the early stages of its formation

*Rev. 2:11, NEB.

when members are defining their strategy.

The mission structure gave us a people to companion us in our individual freedom movement. Everyone struggles to break away from the oppressive inner structures that make us all prisoners of one kind or another. We need a people to journey with us out of our own Egypt into the broad land that is promised to all who believe in Him. "The Son will make you free." The expression of our own freedom will, in the end, be the only credible statement that each of us makes on freedom. Some will be freed for work in ghettos, others to strive for justice in county jails, in halls of government, on boards of industry, or in the writing of a poem.

Arts and Mission

One mission made up of artists was called The Alabaster Jar. Those who labored out of guilt or to satisfy some inner Pharaoh asked what all the "entertainment" had to do with mission and the liberation movement. "After all, we, too, could do a little writing or painting if we didn't have the poor so much with us."

While it is true that not many artists have made profound statements on social issues, the reason may be that we have not allowed them to live in the midst of the people of the God of the freedom movement. It is so much easier to believe in what one can see, and anyway, who really can know what an artist does with all his or her time? Moreover, artists forsake themselves for fear they are betraying the community. I have a friend, a photographer, who says that sometimes when she has spent long hours in the darkroom she is seized with a panicky feeling, "What if there is no one there when I open the door?" I have kindred thoughts when I have done a piece of writing over a long period of time. I open my eyes and observe that life has gone on without me, and there is the dread feeling that never again will I be able to be "in on" things.

By its very name, The Alabaster Jar mission group told us it is all right to follow call even when one is full of self-doubt and is troubled about wasting a "one-time life." They reminded us that we did not have to turn out to be another Picasso or Solzhenitsyn—that we were not called to be successful. Rather we were called to be faithful and to share in the being of the Creator.

No one can know in advance how one will be used, or when, or what one's life will count for in the long run. The young Pablo Casals, while pouring his life energy into years of practice on the cello, could not guess that when Franco came to power, he would stop playing for three years, and that the silence would be heard throughout Spain as if the streets were full of demonstrators. But then, not every artist is called to take up a social or political cause. When the need for bread is met we discover that we have other hungers, and none so deep as the hunger to be understood. The artist helps us to interpret, understand and communicate feeling. When the artist is successful we are led into communion with ourselves and with the world, and the solitary work becomes a communal work. For want of this we walk on parched land.

Implementing Mission Structure

Despite their diversity in outward form, all the missions were ways of casting nets. Ministers struggling with renewal in their own congregations often asked

Gordon Cosby, "If you were in a conventional church situation, what would you do to structure the congregation for renewal?"

He answered then as he still does, "What I am doing now. I would preach Sunday after Sunday on my understanding of the nature of the church. I would preach to the limit of my vision—put into words what it is that I see. I would state the disciplines that are essential if one is to have a relationship with the Holy One—God's anointed One, and have one's life changed by him. And then I would sound a call for the mission that caught my own heart. I would urge others to do the same. After that I would spend the major part of my time just sitting around talking with those who made response to see what would emerge. This sometimes means we let a lot of worthy things go undone."

I put a similar question to the wife of the janitor of the building that we were restoring, "How do you think we can engage the people in this building in the movement to restore the city?" Her response was like Gordon's, "I think we should call them all together and sit around and talk." Now it was our turn to wonder whether we could take the time, for there were no locks on front doors, mailboxes were pried open as soon as they were fixed, the neighborhood received its heroin shots in the basement, and leaking pipes, garbage and roaches were everywhere.

The woman said in her way what the educator Paulo Friere said in his way: "Critical and liberating dialogue, which presupposes action, must be carried on with the oppressed at whatever the stage of their struggle for liberation. Attempting to liberate the oppressed without their reflective participation in the act of liberation is to treat them as objects which must be saved from a burning building; it is to lead them into the populist pitfall and transform them into masses which can be manipulated."*

Gordon tells ministers that their major difficulty in implementing the small group concept will be in trying to justify the time they give to the encouragement of one little group when there is so much work that could be done. "For most of us," he says, "it seems an unconscionable amount of time. We cannot get hold of the fact that the process is sometimes as slow as it is, and we become discouraged even when real growth is taking place. We have no perspective when we try to envision what it means for a community to come into existence. We live under the tension of our own expectations and the expectations of those who are sometimes outright hostile because we are spending our time with a group of unlikely souls when we ought to be taking care of the shut-ins, or the youth, or the elderly. Our congregations are not going to take seriously their responsibility if we ourselves do not take with full seriousness the ministry of the laity."

Another area that Gordon emphasizes in talking with ministers is the need to relinquish control. A staff that feels it necessary to be in control cannot allow things to just happen. "No matter how large a congregation—four or five thousand members—if kept under central authority, it will always be a very limited operation."

The small group structure is threatening because it generates work for which we have no clear guidelines but, when you think about it, it is not nearly as threatening as a congregation with no shared responsibility and no shared life.

The small group is not the discovery of Gordon Cosby, or of anyone else. Christ gave us this model. It was he who had the first mission group. He chose twelve. He

*Pedagogy of the Oppressed, (The Continuum Publishing Corporation, New York, N.Y., 1986) p. 52.

sent them out by twos. He stayed with them for three years when he must surely have been tempted to add to the little band, to sub-divide, and thus to increase the scope of his ministry. Intuitively rather than consciously Gordon has followed this model. A mission group is not brought into existence without a spiritual director and a moderator. We often feel more comfortable with team teaching. More of us are also coming to believe that any group that stays together for less than a three-year period can make neither marked progress in its inward journey nor significant strides toward fulfillment of its mission in the world.

There was a time when, asked to comment on the success of the groups, Gordon Cosby was quick to say that he had the distinction of having presided at the burial of more small groups than had any other minister in the country. Today he would have less reason to make such a claim, for the death of a group is a less frequent occurrence. Groups still go out of existence for varied reasons: when the work is accomplished; when a new form or organization is needed; when leadership does not emerge in sufficient strength; or when the Spirit with its unifying force is absent. Over the years, however, a structure for corporate mission has been evolved that nurtures the inwardness of the group members and, at the same time, enables each one in the group to exercise his or her gift of leadership. The result is a deepening and expanding of the ministry of the group.

2

Therefore, My Sisters, My Brothers

From the day The Church of The Saviour came into existence it has been changing and evolving. In the spring of 1976, we found ourselves engaged in the living of a new Easter. Each day had put before our eyes sights to disturb our sleep and inform our days.

Paulo Friere, who has been a spiritual guide for so many, wrote:

> The process of conscientization leaves no one with his arms folded. It makes some unfold their arms. It leaves others with a guilt feeling, because conscientization shows us that God wants us to act. As I conscientize myself, I realize that my brothers who don't eat, who don't laugh, who don't sing, who don't love, who live oppressed, crushed, and despised, who are less each day, are suffering all this because of some reality that is causing it. And at that point I join in the action historically by genuinely loving, by having the courage to commit myself (which is no easy thing!) or I end up with a sense of guilt because I know I am not doing what I know I should... I can't live my peace without commitment to men, and my commitment to men can't exist without their liberation, and their liberation can't exist without final transformation of the structures that are dehumanizing them. There is only one way for me to find peace: to work for it, shoulder to shoulder with my fellow men.*

When the seventh year—the year with the sacred number that has come to symbolize wholeness—came

*The Ladoc "Keyhole" Series, #I, p.9

around once again in our own congregation, Gordon
Cosby, founder, leader, spiritual father, and brother for
The Church of The Saviour community since its founding, made a statement to the Council that was to involve
us in a radically new structuring of our life. His words
came at the close of a long meeting:

> I have just time to raise a few questions concerning
> my own sense of call, which is intimately related to the
> whole community. I have come to the place where it
> is not possible to carry out responsibly what I have
> traditionally been doing and also to help create new
> structures that have to do with people at the point of
> oppression. Ever since I can remember I have felt this
> as a claim on my life, a claim that has deepened with
> every new mission.
>
> With each step the community has taken it has
> grown in numbers. When it averaged between 60 and
> 70 members we went through a time of redefining
> our corporate life. Now we have 110 members and
> 40 intern members, and much more demanding
> structures, many of which have themselves become
> centers of life.
>
> As the membership has grown and the missions
> have expanded the time demand on us all has in-
> creased. The questions raised with me are: "What is
> the reasonable size? When does a community become
> so large that it cannot operate on the basis of human
> dimensions? How big should administrative units
> be?" We must look at the issue of whether as a
> totality we are larger than we should be. Do we want
> to go the traditional way of pulling in more staff? I
> have these questions as a pastor. My guess is that Bill
> Branner as treasurer has them in the financial area.

Can we keep on stretching without affecting the quality of work to which we are called?

I do not feel that it is right for me to take time from new structures that we are just beginning to develop. Have I a right to withdraw energy from these to pastor the whole, and do any of us have this right? Or can we discover ways together to move into the future without losing our richness or diversity? Is it possible that we can divide into different combinations cohering around different worship centers and, in the process of creating the new, not lose that which we value? There are many, many people in the life of this community with rare gifts of leadership that are not being used. Is it possible that we can have The Church of The Saviour at Massachusetts Avenue with its council, worship, and mission groups cohering around it; another on Columbia Road, cohering around The Potter's House; another around Dayspring?

Or is that not the way to go? Should some leave and just go out while the main body remains intact? I think we have to raise all these questions—bring them into full consciousness. Otherwise we grow larger and larger and struggle to hold it all together and what happens, happens by default.

I am sensing an inability to be faithful to my call and also faithful to the structures that we now have. I am recognizing a developmental stage which can be exciting, if we do not decide to hang on—if we can look at it together. It will be difficult because there is the difficult question, "What is my place in it?" But we can work with it, struggle with it, and trust that the same Spirit which brought us to this point will still be around. We as an organization have been blessed, and my guess is that leadership may be developed at an even deeper level than we have known it.

I am not saying that I have any time schedule, or that I have a master plan, and know how to do it. I am saying that if we ask for the Holy Spirit, pray about it and talk about it, we may discover what is next for us, and that it could be a tremendously exciting and helpful time in our life.

That brief statement was to alter the life of The Church of The Saviour as had no other event in its history. Others were also sensing that change was needed. The small mission groups had flourished. The membership had grown to 120 in number, but that was deceptively small. Each of the groups had intern members and in addition a large periphery of people who gathered around them. The housing group had bought two slum apartment houses. These had literally become their parishes. Other groups were equally involved in ministry. We had the distinct feeling of having grown too large and of being flung out in too many places. Communication was breaking down. Some had suggested adding more staff to try to keep it all together, but that never felt quite right.

When Gordon made his statement it fell on hard as well as churned-up soil. There was no time for discussion at that council meeting, but in the days to come it became abundantly clear that we were moving into the eye of a major transition crisis. The conversation centered around "splitting up" and "dividing." Though we strove for a more positive expression of the issues we were confronting, these words were often injected into the conversation and best described what many of us were feeling. If some felt a kind of terrible and hidden threat, others were stimulated by the proposal and found it full of exciting possibilities. A few bold ones began to respond to the challenge by wondering about themselves in places of leadership. While some imaginatively tried out new roles, others grew angry; still others, depressed, gave the matter no attention at all as though it would go away if properly ignored. One of our activists said, "Why don't we just do our grief work and get on with it?" The reply was that grief has its stages, and denial and anger are in its cycle.

Were size and complexity the bases of our problems, or might they be merely contributing factors? Some felt that, as the groups had developed an autonomous life, we had failed to be in dialogue with each other, failed to wait for one another, failed to keep our covenant of prayer. They argued that repentance should precede a change in structures. Mixed with feelings of joy and adventure were feelings of betrayal and hurt. In the early days of our deliberations a few even felt that they had given their lives to build a community the nature of which they had not fully understood. Family of faith, unlimited liability, brothers and sisters, life together, bearing one another's burdens, the unity of the Body, one part not held in more esteem than the other—these were all concepts that had nurtured and sustained our lives and given to us a sense of safety that had issued in creativity, love of change, and zest for risk-taking. Those qualities had flourished in us, enabling us to embrace all kinds of holy insecurity. Having believed in the permanency of a particular community, we found it dreadfully painful to learn that this community was without a permanent home—literally a people in search of a city that was to come.*

*Heb. 13:14, NEB.

One father recounted the response of his children. His son complained, "Why haven't you asked the children? We talked about it in my mission group and we don't want to change." His little girl's question was, "Daddy, who will get Gordon?"

The struggle of the children reflected that of older, wiser souls. Perhaps because this new Exodus awakened old fears of abandonment, we were not as sure that the call to build a world of justice and caring should be taken with so much seriousness. It was one thing to talk about these things and quite another to Passover ourselves from one way of life to another.

Freud had said woe to the person who tries to replace the charismatic leader. What about this leader of ours who was trying to replace or displace himself? How did we deal with all the wild clamorings that had been set in motion within and around us? What did we, who were no longer children, do with feelings of dependency that lingered on, the need and quest for a spiritual father and mother that every soul harbors? Night and day there had walked in our midst a man who had no limits around his giving, whose outpouring of life and spirit had energized our own lives and illuminated ordinary events. Who would do this for us now? Could we do it for ourselves? Would we give up our own missions and calls and set off for the ghetto after the loved leader, or could we tap some inner strength to choose our own way, claim our own very different paths? How much of the courage and faith that we thought was ours really belonged to him?

We did not always know when we were defending what should be held onto, deepened and extended, or when we were falling into the sin of wanting to perpetuate an institution that, unlike the structures of the world, could not be concerned about enduring, but only about dying, death, and rebirth. We dreaded being "among those who shrink back and are lost," but we were uncertain that we were among those who "have the faith to make life our own."* What did it mean at this stage of our corporate life to be a pilgrim people? Merton speaks about the journey of faith from the security of what is known to the insecurity of what is unknown. We recalled how Abraham was led out from a place he called home, where normalcy prevailed and structures could be counted on to give stability, to a place that was known surely only in the words of Yahweh.

Gradually dark clouds moved away, we began to talk less about what had been, and to look with hope to the future. We spoke more about small liberating communities that would be less encumbered by problems of maintenance, and where large amounts of time usually given to maintaining the unity and healthy functioning of a large organism could flow into the building of small communities of caring in which people could easily find a place, could grow and stretch, and be given a new name. Ever so slowly we began to speak of the New Land to which we were being called, and to learn once more to name Abraham as the father of our faith.

Eight of our members were chosen by the community and "sent out" to explore the New Land. They were asked to report back to the Council on what its shape might be and how the new Exodus might be made. The meetings of that group, called the New Land's Servant Group, were long and arduous. Some knew from the beginning where they were headed and how to go. They did not hide well their impatience with those who were uncertain of the Way, whose heads told them one thing and their feelings another. Among our number

*Heb. 10:39, NEB.

were also those who were process-oriented, and their way clashed with those who operated in a highly intuitive way. Some wanted more prayer and less talk; others, more talk and less prayer. A few wanted to name all the alternatives and to try each on for size, so that we could find out which felt best.

Some were much too literal for fantasy trips of the kind that pictured the church in diaspora—the scattered fellowship. This option included selling all the properties of the church, letting the staff go, and centering our entire focus on building small groups such as our own mission groups. The purpose would be to form communities of the people of God which would come out from the whole of the society and culture in which we live, and form the nuclei of a new society. Like the Assisi community begun by St. Francis, we would endeavor to be a source of light and hope and to live in faithfulness to God's call, with values and a style of life and community which would bear witness to the power of the Gospel. We would not only give up church property, we would share our personal material wealth with the oppressed. We would do so because of a confidence that therein lay the path of our own peace and our own experiencing of the community toward which we were journeying. We could show forth in our life together a way of human fulfillment and true liberation that might become a model for the world to insure survival for all humankind in the decades ahead. Those of us who lived our way deeply into this option saw the growth of such communities throughout the country—even the world— each committed to a common discipline and the encouragement and support of each other. Once a year, or once every seven years, we would meet together for a time of common sharing that would last for seven days.

Like a special "order," the number of such groups would increase.

Such a fantasy was too threatening for some of us to live with for too long. We put it aside, knowing in our hearts that whatever the way we chose as a community, issues had been raised that would have to be dealt with in the future.

Any small group is in some way our whole world in microcosm. In the small group we recreate the experiences and relationships that we have in other combinations of persons. The Jungian analyst, Eleanor Bertine, wrote: "A new world order looms in the dense mists, and the great world-struggle is carried on in miniature within the narrow frame of a little club."* To the small group we bring the hopes, fears, wishes, conflicts, projections, and expectations that move all the time in each of our beings. Those elected by the Council to the New Land's Servant Group found this painfully true. We had to struggle for unity. Sometimes courageously and sometimes, because we could not prevent it, we let our clay feet stick out for everyone to see. In the marriage ceremony Gordon Cosby will often say to the new wife and husband, "I charge each of you to grow to that place where each derives major satisfaction from giving satisfaction to the other." This is a charge that the church might well make to the members of each new group that forms.

After months of meeting, the New Land's Servant Group was sent on a two-day retreat. At our Dayspring Retreat Center amid the surroundings which had so often opened our lives and hearts at new levels to God's word for our individual pilgrimage, we began to sense together beckonings for our corporate way to the New Land.

*Jung's Contribution to Our Time, The Collected Papers of Eleanor Bertine, (J.P. Putnam's Sons for C. J. Jung Foundation, 1967) p. 124.

56

Hart Cowperthwait

**Dayspring, home of many ministries and of the Retreat
Center that nurtures our lives in reflection and contemplation.**

Frank Cresswell

The porch of the Lodge of the Carpenter.

Our retreat at Dayspring began on Sunday evening
with a communion supper. Every group session was
followed by several hours of silence in which to reflect on
what had been said, to listen to God's word and direction.
All the meals were in silence except for readings from
devotional classics. Every new meeting began first with a
sharing of feelings, and then reflections, insights and hints
of the New Land. Moving within this structure our fears
receded. We began to see in concert with each other the
creative possibilities inherent in small sister communities.
We began to let go of familiar ways and familiar landscapes,
to take up once again the never predictable journey of a
tent-dwelling people.

Wes Michaelson, who had been the scribe of all our
meetings, penned the report which was presented at the
next meeting of the Council. In part it read:

Our call must be our starting point. That call is to be
a community centered in resolute faithfulness to Jesus
Christ. It is to be his new community—those who are
his body, molded by his Spirit. To build such a community of faith is our abiding call and revolutionary action.

That call encompasses the marks which our community has discovered through its history to be true and
essential to its identity as God's people: the corporate
commitments of spiritual discipline, the nurture of
mission groups as primary crucibles of community, inner
healing, growth and transformation of our lives into true
maturity in Christ, and the sacrificial outpouring of our
life together in mission to the brokenness of the world.

We believe that our call as a community has four
directions: First, to Christ's church throughout the
world; we are part of the ecumenical church, and want to
give ourselves to its life. Second, to the stranger in

our midst; we are called to bring Christ's love to all those whose lives intersect at any point with ours. Third, to the poor and oppressed of this world. Fourth, to the building of our own common life; all else must flow from our call to be God's people, celebrating and nurturing ourselves as Christ's Body.

The Servant Group for the New Land repeatedly focused on three elements which describe our community's current situation: the size and complexity of our present corporate structures, the overburdening of our pastoral leadership, and the lack of full faithfulness to our covenant.

On our retreat, we further expressed our view of the issues before the community: multiplicity of demands resulting in confusion, dissipation of energy, and erosion of the sense of community.

Our task, then, is to discover structures which will better enable us to live out our corporate call. These structures should provide us with a sense of clarity, new and focused energy for outward mission and inward growth and a deeper sense of Christian community.

We believe that those structures can best be created by the formation of sister communities, each of which will function as a separate congregation, comprised of various clusters of the twenty-two existing mission groups in The Church of The Saviour. These congregations would be bound by deep spiritual ties because of their common parentage, but would be legally and organizationally independent. They would be separate churches, closely linked by history, ongoing fellowship, and potentially interlinking missions.

All mission groups, and thus the entire church membership, would probably find their lives lived out in the context of one of these communities.

The New Land's Servant Group would recommend then, that the existing Church of The Saviour be reconstituted into at least three or more sister communities of faith, with separate leadership, council, budget, organization, worship, and membership.

Such an action would restore clarity to our structures and purposes of corporate life, would enable new energies and creativity to be released for the work of the Kingdom and the deepening of our life in Christ, and the context for us all to experience and build deeper Christian community. The bonds of spiritual kinship and cooperative mission which would be nurtured between these sister communities could, and we hope would be extended toward other communities of Christ's people all over the country and all over the world.

The Church of The Saviour has been born, nurtured, and brought into fullness through the ministry of Gordon Cosby. Naturally his relationship to its future is a matter of primary concern. Through his sharing with us, Gordon has made clear that he continues to be called to the whole community, and that he would continue, if desired by any of the sister communities, to encourage the nurture of new leadership within them, and to assist in ministering on behalf of the growth of each whole. We confirm Gordon in this call.

It is our conviction that these directions will enable us to live out more fully our call to be faithful members of Christ's Body.

During the period of the meetings of the New Land's Servant Group our community used a common lectionary made up of those Scriptures that we felt would be helpful to us in our search. We titled it, Readings for Pilgrimage to the New Land. To the best of our abilities we had allowed our "thoughts and purposes" to be sifted by the Word of God. Alternating with long stretches of unfaith when we worried about ourselves and where we were going were other times when we touched the glory of being among those who have a vision for the earth.

In the days that followed the report to the Council, many of us felt a new kind of solitariness. We were not lonely in any usual sense of that word. We had never had so many meetings, engaged in so many conversations, or had so little time "to ourselves." But in the midst of it we sometimes fell silent. In the long pauses we searched faces to discover kindred souls with whom we might share painful feelings of aloneness. In the end we even drew apart from the faithful friend to become Kierkegaard's "solitary individual," the one who stands alone before God, and comes face to face with his or her own "eternal responsibility." It is one thing to grapple for the corporate form of one's group or community, and another to become the solitary one who struggles for one's own destiny and vocation. Only that person who confronts each day the everlasting responsibility of being an individual can become a true builder of community.

Members of our congregation began to sound calls for the formation of new sister communities or faith communities as we more often call them. Before the year was out six new church communities emerged.

One community formed around The Potter's House and its ministry through a coffee house and book store; another around Jubilee Housing and its commitment to provide safe and affordable housing for the poor. Those issuing the call for the Dayspring Church were committed to spiritual renewal and to caring for the land that The Church of The Saviour had purchased in 1953 as a place of retreat and renewal. Over the years Dayspring had nurtured us in the contemplative life, and the members of the new faith community wanted it to continue as a center where all who touched its life would become more deeply rooted in God and live more fully in covenant with the earth and all sentient beings. The Eighth Day focused its talents and energy on being truly polycultural—open to the insight and inherited wisdom of all the world's cultures. The Seekers initially gathered around innovative worship services and a commitment to fully value and support the spiritual journeys of children. Dunamis, the sixth community, emerged to work with persons at the point of their vocations with an emphasis on those carrying political responsibility.

All these calls to new faith communities were issued by the brave in our midst. The rest of us often seemed to be milling around or engaged in a kind of fervent waiting on God. No one was left sitting on the sidelines. Everyone was engaged in a passionate way. We were looking at ourselves and our missions with a critical absorption, seeking as best we could to discover where God was calling us.

3

The New Land

To some of us the move into faith communities seemed
a bit crazy. It came not at a point of decline to save, as it
were, a sinking ship, but at what seemed to be the prime
of our life. We were rich in missions and rich in friends
and influence.

Once we had tossed all of our thriving fellowship
groups of prayer, study, and worship into the air in the
hope that they would come down as mission groups.
Now, in another reckoning of the years, we had dis-
solved the church itself in the hope that it would be
born again as a number of small church communities—
the new wineskins for the new wine that flowed
in us.

We know so little about the seventh year that we often
experience it as the end rather than as the burial with
Christ that we may be born to the new. But maybe that
is the way it has to be. Maybe it seemed like the end to
Jesus when he descended into the depths of the earth.
In any case some of us looked like sad sacks that winter.
I would like to describe us as sad pilgrims, but we didn't
feel like pilgrims on any path toward a new land. In fact
some thought we were witnessing the end of the community that we had carried as a newborn and watched
over tenderly through all the years of its growing.

Perhaps we were too cowardly, or too wounded by
other losses, or perhaps we were the ones who bonded
more deeply, or were more informed by the feminine in
ourselves. A few even left for good. They may have
found more comfortable structures, or it may be that,
like Lot's wife, they turned to salt.

Lot's wife. Our fathers did not even give her a name.

64

They simply looked on her as one who had refused the call. Not until our age would a woman sing her song:

The just man followed then his angel guide
Where he strode on the black highway, hulking
    and bright;
But a wild grief in his wife's bosom cried,
Look back, it is not too late for a last sight

Of the red towers of your native Sodom, the square
Where once you sang, the gardens you shall mourn,
And the tall house with empty windows where
You loved your husband and your babes were born.

She turned, and looking on the bitter view
Her eyes were welded shut by mortal pain;
Into transparent salt her body grew,
And her quick feet were rooted in the plain.

Who would waste tears upon her? Is she not
The least of our losses, this unhappy wife?
Yet in my heart she will not be forgot
Who, for a single backward glance, gave up her life.*

    I do not remember our caring well for one another in those days. It could not have been otherwise. In every transition period we have ourselves on our hands. Visitors who came to be with us at that time sensed our confusion and fatigue.
    Once again we learned that terrible uncertainty is a primary characteristic of a transition period. The old is gone—lost forever. There is no going back, but the new has not yet been secured. Even those who glimpsed it with the inward eye could not be fully sure that they

*Anna Akhmatova, "Lot's Wife," (translated from Russian by Richard Wilbur), *The Penquin Book of Women Poets*. edited by Carol Cosman, Joan Keefe and Kathleen Weaver, 1979, p. 191.

would find a place for themselves in that far country which sometimes seemed fair and inviting and at other times full of giants, making them feel as grasshoppers. Abraham journeyed by stages and, for his descendants as for him, it is always a walk of faith.

Another thing about the crises of individuals and institutions—they always activate all of our unconscious conflicts. Small wonder that individuals as well as institutions settle for mediocrity, even deadness, rather than get down into the churning waters where old anxieties and guilts are stirring, and where we must face the dependencies, loves and vanities of earlier years. It is as though every seven years God gives to each of us an opportunity to work once again, from a more mature place, on unresolved issues of love and hate, of fear and loss. That work which is the work of salvation is always done in fear and trembling.

In the next year each of the new communities had to do the hard labor of pitching tents and driving down stakes, often requiring seemingly interminable meetings in which new structures had to be hammered through. We also had to do the painful inner work of finding new territory within ourselves on which to stand.

Since the communities had no paid leadership or ordained clergy in charge, the identifying of gifts became an urgent matter. Many of us agreed to preach, who in our wildest imaginations had never thought we would. We found the courage because there was no professional to do it. Soon we were all taking turns and surprised to find our little congregations growing in number.

We made mistakes, but grew practiced in getting up and going on, learning to be healers of each other, accepting and forgiving each other and in the process discovering each other. It never would have happened if the church had not been based since its inception on the New Testament concept of the priesthood of all believers. In his first brochure on the church Gordon Cosby had quoted the counsel of the writer and Quaker leader, Elton Trueblood, "No passengers—everyone a member of the crew."

A church cannot take seriously the concept of the priesthood of all believers without conceiving of itself as a seminary for the training of the laity for the priesthood. The School of Christian Living had been doing just that through all the years—training its members to be servant leaders.

The movement to the New Land could not have been made without a deep trust in the capacity of lay persons to be priests, but that trust would have been sadly misplaced had there not been at the heart of the community one hundred twenty lay persons disciplined in the devotional life and trained to be servant leaders. The risk was there, nonetheless, because one never fully becomes a leader until one has found the courage to lead.

I am not a writer because I have read books on writing. I am a writer because I write.

We are not teachers because we have learned teaching methods. We are teachers when day after day through our speaking and our listening we impart the knowledge that each one of us is a teacher.

We are not religious persons because we read the Bible, pray, and say the proper words. We are persons of faith when we are exercising the capacity that each of us has to be a priest—when we are about the business of healing the divisions that exist within us, between us, and among us. The strange thing about our being priests is that we heal ourselves as we engage in binding up the wounds of others.

At the heart of each of the new communities was a
School of Christian Living, offering the same five classes
that had always been required for membership: Old
Testament, New Testament, Doctrine, Ethics, and Christian Growth. Each of them would teach self-knowledge.
Training for the priesthood, when all is said and done, is
learning to be one's self. And priesting or serving is creating hospitable structures where people can feel safe enough
to do the arduous work of becoming themselves—the icons
of God that they are intended to be. That is all that we
have to do in life—be ourselves, connect to that deep place
in us from which living waters flow.

In addition to having its own school and leadership,
each of the new churches had its own council, budget
and mission groups. An Ecumenical Counsel, made up
of two representatives from each of the communities,
was elected to deal with matters of interest to all of
the communities.

Now fourteen years have gone by since the new
churches were formed. Dunamis, the smallest of them,
floundered along for a number of years, and finally
became too bogged down in interpersonal problems to
continue. The other communities had their own struggles,
but managed to put down deep roots and to flourish.
In time four new communities were born, so that today
the faith communities of The Church of The Saviour are
nine in number.

While existing under the same umbrella and bound by
the same covenant, each community has its own indi-
viduality. One cannot visit one of the church communities
and know what the others are like. Even the worship
services are different, though they may be held in the
same place. The Eighth Day Community, which worships
on Sunday morning in The Potter's House, is full of

young musicians who from time to time bring their violins, or guitars and cymbals. Their announcements are sometimes as long as their sermons. This community, while utterly serious about its disciplines and missions, seems to know more about play than the others. It is not at all unusual for thirty or more of the congregation to take off for a week's hike up a mountain or for a biking trip through a nearby state. Those of us in the the other churches who hear about these things often wonder if we are not missing out on something important.

The Jubilee Church, which has its worship service in The Potter's House on Monday nights is more indigenous to the neighborhood and a wild mix of everyone—black and white, the sane and demented, rich and poor, the very young and the old, Jew and Gentile, the deeply committed and those who wander in just to eat the simple meal that is served. Some say this may be the look of the Kingdom Church.

The service held by The Potter's House Church in the same room on Wednesday nights is a different experience. Going through the doors of The Potter's House on that night is almost like stumbling on a gentle clearing in a jungle. Even the sirens in the street seem to bounce off the silence in the walls. Each week a different member gives a brief sermon which is then pondered around the coffee tables over a communion meal of cheese and fruit.

Not many blocks away, but deeper into the inner city, is The New Community Church. Its home is a partially restored four-story house on a battered and stricken street where discarded furniture and old boxes litter the broken sidewalks and half the houses are boarded up. Once the street might have been called Godforsaken, so

David Welsh

The street scene outside The Potter's House

lacking was it in any evidence of divine grace.

I will not try to describe even briefly each of the worship services of the different faith communities, but I cannot resist telling you about the Sunday when I worshipped with The New Community. The Scripture was Luke 19:1-10—the story of Zacchaeus who climbed a sycamore tree to catch a glimpse of Jesus. You will remember that when Jesus reached that spot he looked up and saw him in the tree and told him to hurry down because he wanted to stay at his house that night. The crowd complained because Zacchaeus was the senior tax collector and wealthy to boot. But Jesus told his taunters that he had come to seek out and save what was lost.

Jim Dickerson, the founder and pastor of The New Community, reminded the small congregation of the tree that had grown in the lot alongside their house. The tree, he recalled, had been a favorite hangout for the neighborhood. People could do all kinds of things behind the tree and no one could see them. The yard was also a dumping place for tires and trash and drug syringes. Church members would come to Jim and ask, "What are you going to do about the tree?" What they meant by that was, "What are you going to do about the people who gather under the tree?" One day half the tree was gone. It had been split down the middle and half of it carted away. No one knew what had happened. Some said it was lightning; others thought it might have been wind or fire.

Jim passed pictures around so that we could see what had befallen the tree, how the rubble-strewn yard looked when it was there, and how tidy it looked now that the tree was gone. He pointed out that no one was more lost than some of the people who had gathered around that tree. Even the drug dealers whom we hated were the ones for whom Jesus came. "They are my enemies," Jim said, "so according to the Gospel message they are the ones I am to love."

After this brief sermon members in the congregation were asked to volunteer for parts in a two-page play on "Zacchaeus in the Tree." A small black child volunteered for the part of Jesus and a tall white man for the part of the short Zacchaeus. We, in the congregation, were asked to play the role of "the crowd." Despite the casting, or maybe because of it, when the presentation was over everyone had a better idea of what the story of Zacchaeus was all about.

Jim then asked Greg Campbell to come forward and present the drawing for the fence and gate that would be across the front of the yard where the tree had stood. When he held up the large, mounted design it was a wondrously professional drawing depicting Jesus reaching out to Zacchaeus who was in the tree and being jeered at by onlookers. The response in the room was one of awe, perhaps because it was hard for this particular gathering of people to imagine that the little yard on their bruised and wounded street was to hold so much beauty.

At Jim's request Greg told the room of entranced worshippers how the drawing came to be. He said that he did ornamental iron work and that soon after the New Community house had been purchased, Jim had called to request that he come by and put bars on the windows. "When I arrived," he said, "I couldn't believe the sight I saw. The rooms were knee-deep in trash that included bottles, broken glass, and discarded drug needles. The smell was awful. When Jim told me that it was going to be a church I couldn't imagine it. I had never been in a place more repulsive. It was revolting.

My helper and I were scared, and we don't scare easily."

After Greg had finished barring the windows he didn't come back until Jim called and asked him to make a fence and small gate for the narrow yard to the right of the house. When he came to take the measurements he again couldn't believe his eyes—only now it was because of the transformation that had taken place inside the house. The rooms were clean and full of light and color, and the touch of the artist's brush was everywhere. When Greg delivered the finished iron gate, to everyone's surprise, it held a cross with a magnificent descending dove of hammered, polished steel at its center. The gate graced the whole street and became a source of conversation. People wanted to know what the dove meant and why it was descending instead of going up.

Jim, who had never thought art deserved much attention, found himself enthralled by the gate and the dove, and the wonder in the eyes of his neighbors. He telephoned Greg and told him that he wanted an iron railing and gate for the larger yard to the left of the house where the tree had stood. Inscribed on it were to be the words, "The Son of Man has come to seek out and save what was lost."*

Jim found in Greg a ready and eager artisan. "I had always tried to tell myself, " Greg said, "that bars are useful, that bars keep people and their possessions safe, but I could not put myself into my calling. Talking to Jim that day I knew I was going to be able to express myself and my love of God through my work, and that this was the meaning of 'calling.'"

That was not the end of Greg's story. Before the images that burned in him could be put into steel and iron they had to undergo the discipline of the designer's

*Lk. 19:10, Jer.

Elizabeth O'Connor

The gate and the dove

74

art in which he was unpracticed. It happened that, several weeks before, a Russian immigrant named Nikoli Pakhomov had come to him asking for work. "He told me," said Greg, "that he was an architect and had worked for Gorbachev and many of the Russian leaders, but could not find work in this country. I did not know why he came to me, since I have only a small business, but I hired him that day."

After visiting with Jim, Greg had returned to the job where he and Nicoli were working and told him about the church and the new commission he had for an iron fence and gate that would tell the story of Zacchaeus. Although Nikoli spoke little English, had never read the Bible and knew nothing of Zacchaeus, he grasped immediately the importance of what Greg was telling him. A utility man who was laying a gas line close by overheard their stumbling and animated conversation and offered to loan Nicholi a Russian edition of the Bible that he had at home. After Nicoli read the story of Zacchaeus, he and Greg planned the iron fence and gate and Nicoli created the design that they would together put into iron and steel.

The service ended with the singing of an original song that had the refrain:

Come down, Zacchaeus! I see you in that tree,
Hurry, Zacchaeus, today you will be free.*

The song seemed especially fitting since creativity is born of our freedom and when dedicated to the good is always a liberating act. I would not tell this story of Greg and Nicoli if all the communities did not abound in art, and music and poems, and a growing awareness that each and every one has the exalted vocation to

* Veneta Mason, New Community Church, 1991.

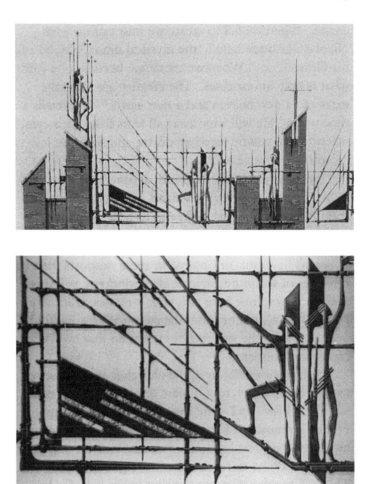

**A photograph of Nikoli Paphomov's drawing and a detail
showing the taunters of Zaccheus**

create. When we fail to create we miss out on what Nicolas Berdyaev called "the mystical drama of God and his Other One." When we create we become one with what is holy in ourselves. The creative act bears the mark of "a new heaven and a new earth." It foretells a time when "He will wipe away all tears from their eyes," when "there will be no more death, and no more mourning or sadness."*

One art work seems to inspire another. Some days I think that in a future time visitors will come to the communities simply to look, and to hear by chance, or so they will believe, the story of the mission groups and their institutions.

Artists have not only placed in these outposts their offerings of sculpture, stained glass windows, paintings and tapestries, they have also taught classes in art, story-telling, poetry, quilting and dance to children and old people, and to the sick and homeless, so that everywhere creativity abounds.

The institutions born of the churches are themselves works of art. They, too, impart spirit-energy and make way for others. As I write this, the newest, Lazarus House, a renovated four-story building that will accom-modate eighty-one homeless men and women has opened its doors to receive the first eight residents. They tell me that they are dancing in the halls for joy, which is not hard to imagine if one has been to Lazarus House. When the building was dedicated we all had a chance to walk on the thick carpets with their designer patterns, and to stand in the rooms with their pastel walls. Each room has the same heavy, wooden furnish-ing, the kind you might find in a retreat house, and its own refrigerator, heating and air conditioning. The single bedrooms, arranged in clusters of six to ten, give

*Rev. 21:1 and 4, Jer.

to men and women used to shelter dorms the unexpected gift of privacy. Each cluster of rooms has a common kitchen, living room, two or three bathrooms, and laundry facilities. They are obviously designed to facilitate the creation of small communities. Part of the covenant of Lazarus House is that residents will participate weekly in support and counseling groups meeting in the staff offices. Church services are already being held in a large community room and are open to all who want to attend.

The dedication of the building was a tearful time. At last everyone could see the fruits of long labor. The funding and renovation of the building were provided by dozens of city businesses and foundations, whose representatives said one after the other that they were ready to do the same thing for another building. The miracle was not only in the beauty of a building that had been uninhabitable for years, but that the gracious rooms were going to provide help and space for once homeless men and women struggling to put their shattered lives back together.

In the entrance hall of Lazarus House is the art work of Lee Porter, a member of the Jubilee Church. It tells the story of the good Samaritan. The wall hanging speaks for the journey that we are all on, and the miracle of love that unexpectedly we found in our hearts for men and women who were once among the earth's outcasts.

The writer, William F. Lynch, believed that "if love is being restored, so is hope, for our greatest hope and wish is to be able to love." This is another of the miracles of the missions. We set out to restore the lives of others and find our own lives redeemed.

Hard to remember back to that time forty years ago when The Potter's House was our only mission. Around one of its tables Jubilee Housing was planned. After the first two apartment houses were renovated and converted into clean and affordable housing for low income families, Jubilee Jobs was formed to help unemployed tenants find the jobs they were so desperately seeking.

A chance visit was behind the story of The Columbia Road Health Services. Allen and Janelle Goetcheus were waiting for a visa to go to Pakistan when they came to visit the The Church of The Saviour and were taken to see Jubilee buildings that were being restored. Knowing that Janelle was a physician, her guides for the day shared with her the health needs of those living in the buildings and neighborhood. She and Allen returned home and, after a number of months, made the decision to go to Washington instead of Pakistan. They were uncertain about what would happen, but they knew they were going to a community that would support their dream of working with some of the poor of the world.

Allen, a gifted United Methodist minister with a major in drama, took a job as manager of The Potter's House, while Janelle worked in a suburban hospital several days a week to help support their household which included three children and a dog. The rest of the time she worked in an inner city clinic and planned Columbia Road Health Services. It first opened in a vacant commercial flat and then moved into space that became available in The Potter's House building. By that time the health team included three doctors, several nurses, a social worker and a receptionist.

Janelle and her colleagues quickly became aware that many of the people they were seeing were living on the streets. The shelters gave them beds at night but during the day they had to walk the streets in all kinds of weather. Some who had a virus when a doctor first saw them would, on their next visit, have pneumonia. Others, released from hospitals with leg fractures, were trying to live on the streets with full leg casts. Still others had been released to shelters after having had major surgery, such as a coronary artery bypass. "Little by little," said Janelle, "we began to know that we could not continue to turn people away after treating them. We needed a place where they could stay until they were well. We also wanted to know our patients in more depth. We wanted not only to do for them—we wanted to be with them."

When a large gift made possible the purchase and renovation of a vacant building that the staff had stood in front of and asked God to give them, three doctors and their families moved in along with their sick and homeless patients. "Be careful what you set your heart on," James Baldwin's grandfather is said to have told him, "because you will surely get it." They named the coveted building Christ House.

Today it is not at all unusual to look into a room and see a doctor's child engaged in an intense game of chess with a friend he has made on the ward, or see the children wander among the tables at the supper hour which, on Thursday nights, is open to visitors. At each plate there is always a Scripture hand-written in calligraphy by a former patient. In the worship time residents share how the verse relates to their lives and experiences. As I listen to them my own fearful heart gains a new perspective and is restored to praise. This seems to be the common experience of visitors. I think of these sharing times when communities fight so fiercely the placement of half-way houses in their neighborhoods. The inner poverty of those self-enclosed streets seems so great and the lives of their citizens so deprived of experience that it is not at all clear who are the rich and who are the poor, who are the well and who are the sick.

One great difficulty, however, arose at Christ House. When you "make real friends with the poor,"* as we are instructed to do, you don't put those friends out into the street, even if they are well. It followed as the night the day, that someone in the faith communities would hear the call to provide transitional housing. In May of 1986, Samaritan Inns put up its first sign on the door of a row house around the corner from The Potter's House, and a year later put its emblem on a second house a few doors away. A third Inn soon followed, and then had come the grand undertaking of Lazarus House, offering less structured and more independent living.

An example of an older, smaller, and more hidden ministry is a Montessori school for very young children conducted in the basement of the first Jubiliee building. Nona Beth Landon, a slender young woman with long braided hair and degrees in music and education, is the founder. For fifteen years she and one of the mothers living in a Jubilee building have been the Pied Pipers for scores of children in the surrounding streets. In time other centers for children, offering tutoring and art programs, opened in the basements of Jubilee apartment buildings. Somewhere in the wonder of it all is Family Place, a home-like, drop-in center for young immigrant mothers and their small children. Its wide range of programs includes social services, counseling, support groups and meals. Completing the cluster of missions is Sarah's Circle, a 36-unit inter-generational housing program with an emphasis on the elderly. Its basement also has a kitchen and drop-in center. Long ago we made the discovery that the basements of old apartment houses are the District of Columbia's richest unexploited real estate.

*Rm. 12:16, Jer.

In the same area, a half-block from where I live, another new mission, Joseph's House, has opened its doors to homeless men with AIDS. The house takes its name from the biblical Joseph who, despised and hated by his brothers, became the one whom God used to save the entire people of God. David Hilfiker, the doctor and founder, who has moved into the house with his wife and children, wrote:

> We envision Joseph's House as a place where the ostracized and hated of society are protected, where their hopes and imaginations are nourished. As the years of American domination and plenty come to an end, and American famine is threatened, the culture's survival is dependent on the visions of those whom it has marginalized. We are hopeful that within this community dreams and visions will be mutually nurtured and offered back to the society.

At a conference where I was talking about this little circle of missions that sustain and support each other, someone spoke up and said, "I'm afraid to come to D.C." Another said, "They do call it the murder capital of the world." Others nodded their heads.

The response was understandable. I know the fragile peace of my own neighborhood, the misery and despair hidden away in the streets we walk every day. Sometimes I am afraid, but more often I am energized by the rich diversity of its people, its hope and vision. "Do you know Adams Morgan?" I asked, thinking I might tell them something about this neighborhood that would change the way they viewed my city.

"Oh yes," said one, "I was there several years ago when the drunk offered the kneeling Jesus a drink and ended up pouring it on his head."

Elizabeth O'Connor

Jimilu's *Servant Christ* is not in some protected corner of a church, but on the sidewalk where people can respond in whatever way they choose. This figure of Jesus is open, vulnerable and inviting. No one is indifferent to finding him in their streets. "He is my friend," a homeless man said to Gordon Cosby, who replied, "and mine, too."

I, too, remembered that time. He was referring to
Jimilu's *Servant Christ*, the bronze figure in front of
Christ House. Jesus is barefoot and looks as though he
might be wearing jeans. He is holding a basin in one
hand; the other is raised in a gesture that invites those
sitting on the benches to have their feet washed. To the
crazed young man, wearing only shoes and shorts, Jesus
must have looked like someone not very different from
himself. He gazed at him for a long, long time, as
though the power in the sculpted piece had grasped
something deep in himself. Later I wondered if he
might have thought that the kneeling figure was a
beggar, pleading for sustenance. In any case, he finally
held the bottle to the mouth of Jesus so that he could
drink from it. When Jesus was unresponsive he poured
some of the contents on his head. After that he stood
back and gave the immovable one a bewildered look.
He finally took the bottle from its brown paper bag and
placed it carefully in the hand of Jesus. The scene
seemed a poignant one to me, and not too different
from the story of the widow and her mite.

"So many times," I told this gathering, "I walk the
streets of Adams Morgan and look up to catch in quite
different scenes a glimpse of the New Jerusalem coming
down out of the skies." On these streets are spoken
the tongues of many lands and still we so often understand what people are saying. Here some of the refugees
of the world have found a safe place to lay their heads,
cradle their babies, and sell their wares from folding
tables and tiny stores. Here the demented can still
wander in and out of our shops. Here some places have
been made for the young and the old. Here the broken
are received and the sick healed. Here the Gospel is
being preached and here, faulted as we are, with our own

griefs heavily upon us, we are bold to say God calls us his people and we know that "his name is *God-with-them*."*

Each of the communities has its own cluster of missions stamped with their own uniqueness, telling stories of struggle, grit and grime, and luminous moments when they were bearers of mercy and grace. Sometimes these missions of the communities, so wondrous to behold, are sorely beset with the problems that we have with ourselves and each other—our small and large betrayals, our competitiveness, our envy, our different and strong opinions of how things ought to be, our rush to get things done or our taking forever, our struggles to control, to have our wills prevail, and on and on—all those petty and serious ways in which we fail to embody the concepts of servant leadership that roll so easily from our tongues. If on some days I question my singing ever the song of the missions, on others I discern the transcendent mystery flowing through all these efforts. The good news is that the glimmering structures prefiguring another world are the work of ordinary folk. If they were the work of the spiritually gifted or of those who had it all together or were especially wise, the rest of us could pass them by, as not relevant to our lives. As it is now, they let us know that all things are possible and that over our darkness is a blanket of forgiveness. They teach us that at the center of our lives are the vast storehouses of untapped resources needed for the restoration of our communities and our world.

In one of the classes in the School of Christian Living, Gordon Cosby told the students:

Every structure in which you work can feel the impact of your presence within it. You might want to begin questioning most of the fundamental assumptions

*Rev. 21:4, Jer.

operating within that structure. At the same time the Church of Jesus Christ ought to be creating literally countless alternative institutions of power incarnating some portion of a Kingdom vision and corporately embodying a more human way of ordering life. There are very few of these radical alternative structures pointing the way to a new society, and saying this is how as a biblical people we live while waiting the coming of Jesus Christ. This is why the Christian church in so many areas of our diseased society has little impact upon the quality of life in America.

These mini institutions must grow out of the biblical vision. And if they grow out of that vision, they will dramatically proclaim a solidarity with the poor, with those who suffer most deeply at the margins of society. These structures will not isolate the poor while serving them. They will recognize that the poor are the true leaders and work alongside them in their struggle for a more just world. They will provide an opportunity for the privileged and de-prived, the rich and the poor to be together—to break down the dividing wall of partition which separates. A structure which serves the poor is one thing; a structure which serves the poor while evoking their gifts and leadership and nourishing genuine friend-ships is quite different—much more significant. Such structures will, by their very nature and being, judge and confront the systems of the world which produce the dehumanizing conditions that we deplore.

Of course, behind every creative work, whether it be a poem or an institution, is boundless sacrifice. This week I made a solemn statement of that sort to Diana Wright, a friend and writer: "All creativity requires sacrifice."

She replied, "Yes, but the meaning of sacrifice is to make sacred." She went on to point out that in Greek tradition the sacrifice had to be willingly made, so that if the animal chosen to be offered up showed resistance, it was let go and another put in its place. I knew that what she said was profound and true. We have to lay down our lives of our own free consent. Otherwise, our offerings, even when they are used, will not hallow the profane or fulfill our human hopes.

As each of the new churches brought into being its own cluster of mission groups, our horizons expanded to include a wider range of concerns such as earthkeeping, our multicultural environment, peace and war, and the nurture of persons in places of government leadership. We go to each other's gatherings around these issues and read each other's newsletters. We also stay in touch through our fund-raising letters. We send these letters not only to friends all over the country, we send them to each other in The Church of The Saviour communities. We respond in various ways to these appeals in accordance with our individual temperaments and maybe in different ways on different days. Sometimes we are burdened by their number, or feel guilty because we are not doing more, but most of us most of the time like receiving them. They keep us close to the heart-beat of the things we care about and want to keep in our prayers, even when we have no money to give.

Some of us go so far as to consider our fund-raising dinners our most festive events—where we hear firsthand the miracle stories that the folk in all the missions have to tell. Of course, there is always a time to make a contribution or a pledge. Since we all manage, somehow, to support each other's missions, one wonders whether the same money is being passed from one pocket to the other; even so, it mysteriously multiplies along the way. Because so many of us at these banquets look a little down-at-the-heel, we constantly amaze ourselves when the gifts are counted to find them always in the thousands. These are added to by people all over the city and all over the country, some of whom have never seen the missions and yet believe.

As new mission groups came into being to deal with issues of racism, education, politics and other large issues, some of us who had been on the periphery of the life in our own congregations, together with some of the "third world" of our city, were able to move in closer to the places where new life was breaking. Some days as we labored together, the very climate came alive with possibility. We began to feel that we could believe in ourselves again, and in the power of the Spirit at work in the world.

Perhaps one of these days we who are city dwellers will give up the myth of our powerlessness, turn around, and move in a new direction. We do not have to sit around immobilized, waiting for help to come. We can learn to care for our society, which in large part means learning to care for our cities. If our streets are to be redeemed we will have to commit our own human and financial resources to that goal. We will have to recover our gifts of faith and hope and endurance, evoke the gifts of other persons, and thus develop leaders and facilitators for the building of a global network of small, disciplined, self-critical groups whose reflection will issue in purposeful action. This is a way to join in the liberation movement that is going on in all the poor countries of the world. We are not the initiators of this movement. Even the suffering ones of the earth are not the initiators, though they are the genuine leaders. The movement is God's as was firmly established when God directed Moses to tell a people in slavery, "I AM has sent me to you."*

In his *Handbook for Small Mission Groups*,** Gordon Cosby describes the nuts and bolts of groups that endeavor to be agents of change in the lives of their members and agents of social change in the world. They might be called compassion groups, which is a name that Michael Lerner uses when he envisions such groups undergirding a mass movement of compassion. I like that name better than mission groups. In our modern society mission might imply making others the objects of charity rather than describing the reciprocal relationships that exist within the groups and with the world.

One of the chief tasks of these groups would be to create safe space in which the members could tell their stories—what has happened to them in the past, what is happening in their hearts in their present life situations, and their dreams, fears and hopes for the future. My own experience as a leader of small therapy groups has utterly convinced me that the person that I come to know I will come to love. As Christians we have the duty to love the person before us with all his or her imperfections, frailties and distorted ways of seeing things. The assignment comes in Holy Scripture, "Those who say, 'I love God,' and hate their brothers or sisters, are liars; for those who do not love a brother or sister whom they have seen, cannot love God whom they have not seen."*** Soren Kierkegaard in one of his many reflections on the Scripture wrote, "*If this is our duty, then the task does not consist in finding—the lovable object; but the task consists in finding the object already given or chosen—lovable, and in continuing to find him*

lovable however changed he is." *   Very little has been
written, however, on how much easier that assignment
becomes when we take the risk of letting each other into
our hearts, find the courage to be authentic for each
other, willing to reveal ourselves, to give up the defenses
and facades behind which we hide. This is always a
journey. It is not as though I can take my life and open
it up for you to see as I choose. The fact is that as I drop
my protective ways, I become known not only to you
but known to myself. More than this, the mystical union
with Christ is dependent upon this knowing.

For this reason our spiritual leaders are beginning to
give emphasis to storytelling—so that we may come to
know ourselves and each other and learn to love. In
such a journey we will discover not only the light that is
in us, but also the darkness, and the tremendous capacity
that each of us has for self-deception. We will always
find it easier to see in others the quest for power, success, and private gain than to recognize these strivings in
ourselves. Those of us working in the outreach programs of the churches are especially in danger of becoming identified with the good that we do. This may be
the reason Jesus said, "Why do you call me good? No
one is good but God alone,"* *   and why James told
those folk in the New Testament church "...confess your
sins to one another, and pray for one another, and this
will cure you."* * *

In small groups we can create the climate and nurture
the trust in which a deep giving of ourselves can happen.
Much more than the confession of our light or our
darkness is involved. What is involved is the recovery of
love, itself, the communion that is the deepest need of
every life, the unlocking of that infinite capacity that
each one has to be a friend and to have a friend. If the

*Works of Love, translated from the Danish by David F. Swenson and Lillian Marvin
Swenson, (Princeton University Press, Princeton, N.J., 1949) p.l29.
** Lk. l8:19, Jer.
***Jm.. 5:l6, Jer.

pilgrim journey is a journey toward freedom, then the liberating work is the freeing of love in me and the freeing of love in you. Unfortunately, this journey which is the foundation of the community in Christ is not well mapped for us, but it is abundantly clear that it is more easily made within a group of twelve or fewer.

The difficulty confronting the churches in the organization of a small group movement is the lack of leadership for such groups. The Scripture says, "Leaders, exert yourselves to lead," but that is hard to do when most of us lack the confidence required to assume this kind of responsibility. We have discovered over the years that even the people who know how to administer churches, banks, corporations, and hospital units have no idea how to nurture a small group so that its members deepen their lives in Christ—learn self-knowledge, how to listen and to care—the deep nurture of the spiritual life so essential for the recovery of vision and passion.

The lack of servant leaders is being experienced in the whole of society. One looks in vain today for those who are using their strengths and gifts and riches on behalf of the common good. In all of our institutions is a yearning for the presence of the fearless ones in whose company we will be able to put aside our own fears and begin to hope and exercise imagination.

In the midst of our own communities a Servant Leadership School has emerged to work with all the issues involved in servant leadership. Located in the Adams Morgan area, the School is surrounded by nine of the missions of the church. The tower building is gracious in design, but the streets themselves and the missions are its extended classrooms. The deepest learnings of our church communities have come from their intermingling with the oppressed of the world, so it is natural that we would want to make that same opportunity available to other church communities. A central understanding of the School is that participants are committed to being in ongoing relationships with oppressed people. In one sense the School is an ecumenical undertaking by Christians from many places who have awakened to the pain and oppression in their own situations, and been given a vision of a more merciful world. They want a place where they can struggle with others for the renewal of their individual lives and institutions. One can imagine that in time the School might become a think tank and a feel tank where Christians from all walks of life will come together to dream and plan and engage in the struggle of the abused and suffering of the earth, and to ask what it means to pitch our tents in their midst.

The Servant Leadership School is not unlike our own Schools of Christian Living except that it is wider in scope and will draw upon the leadership of the larger church, as well as our nine faith communities. The core curriculum is composed of five dimensions: Servant Leadership, Community Building, Spiritual Grounding, Call or Vocation, and Personal Response to Being with the Oppressed. Other courses will help us to work with equally profound areas of our lives, concerns that we did not worry about before we became grown-ups. They include such vast and varied subjects as money, authority and power, social and economic justice, growing old, death and dying, addictions, the education of our feelings and sensibilities.

From our own experience and the teachings of Paulo Freire we have learned that the development of the kind of learning center that we dream about does not happen when educators allow themselves to be set up as the

David Welsh

The doors of The Servant Leadership School open on the neighborhood that is its primary classroom.

dispensers of knowledge to willing disciples. We do not learn to think or to feel by filling our notebooks with the gems of bright minds, though there is, indeed, an important place for that. Our critical faculties, however, and our capacity to take the risk of thinking and acting are developed when educators and educatees engage in dialogue. Those who care about the School must shelter well the dream that it will become a place of dialogue where we struggle together for ways to work with the problems that are threatening to overwhelm our society. The people in the streets surrounding the School will have to be included in that dialogue, because no servant structure of growing and learning can thrive without them. Reflection and contemplation must also be learned and taught for these are the seedbed of all awakenings.

When participants in the School have completed the core curriculum, either through the weekly classes or through weekend workshops, they will be invited to join the Community of Servant Leaders. As these leaders try to incarnate the concepts of servant leadership they will be encouraged and sustained by the evolving study programs, literature and gatherings of the School. The hope is that in time a cadre of servant leaders will bring into being other Servant Leadership Schools and thousands and thousands of small compassion groups where people come together to pray, dream, plan, and take action for a fairer world.

Like our mission groups, these groups will be bound by a common covenant, the purpose of which will be the transformation of individual lives and the transformation of society. The dream of transforming individuals and societies through small groups is radical and very old. It was probably first attempted by Moses when he accepted the counsel of his father-in-law who had observed that he was in danger of burnout if he kept trying to lead a revolution by himself—"It is not right to take this on yourself. You will tire yourself out, you and the people with you...choose from the people at large some capable and God-fearing men, trustworthy and incorruptible, and appoint them as leaders of the people: leaders of thousands, hundreds, fifties, tens."* After Moses we have the model of Jesus, in a more modest way, living out with twelve the concept of servant leadership.

Holding to the narrow way, as life-promising as it may be, has never been easy, and is especially difficult in our market-driven, industrial countries with their emphases on consumption and private gain. Very few today talk about or value solitude, creativity, friendship, dialogue, reflection, political and social action on behalf of oppressed persons—a different way of being in the world. All these possibilities for our lives would be nurtured in the small groups.

From his studies of the mythologies of the world Joseph Campbell gives us the story of the great king, Minos, who could not resist his impulses to acquisition and "became the dangerous tyrant Holdfast—out for himself."** As scandal after scandal unfolds in all the institutions of our society, I have thought of the tyrant Holdfast, but mainly I have thought of him as I am tempted along the way to keep for me and mine the gifts that have been given to me for the common good. One of the emphases of the School will be to make conscious this temptation to acquisition that confronted Christ early in his ministry and confronts each of us all along the way. The servant leader of yesterday is always in danger of becoming the tyrant Holdfast of tomorrow,

*Ex. 18:17, 18, 21, Jer.
* *The Hero with a Thousand Faces (Bollinger Series XVII,Princeton University Press, Princeton, N.J., 1949) p. 15.

unless he or she learns to die in the now. This is what
Christ told us servant leadership was all about—dying and
being born again. It is never only one death. For the
pilgrim person the deaths and births are always many.

When the curriculum of the School has been carefully
considered we must ask again, what is this journey toward
servant leadership? How do we die and be born again of
the spirit? How do we learn to see with new eyes, hear
with new ears, and speak with a new voice? How do we
find wings and fly, become artisans all? Jesus told us that
the kingdom of God is within. The prize of great worth is
hidden in the depths of our own hearts. We must each
learn and teach the secret of this treasure hidden in a field
so that we, ourselves, may be fully alive, the universe
restored and fed, and Christ' s redeeming voice heard
again in our streets and in the streets of the world.